POWER
APPS

To order, call 256-759-7492
Visit http://www.jeremyanderson.org and
www.spiritreign.org

The author assumes full responsibility for the accuracy of
facts and quotations as cited in this book.

Edited by: Tawanna Anderson, Jan Ross, Erin Davis, Katie
Arnette, Traci Anderson, Rita Gains, Twanna Collins &
Jonae Jackson

Cover Design, Interior Design, Illustrations, and
Photographs by: Daryl S. Anderson Sr., Founder and CEO
of Spirit Reign Communications

Photographs by Aaron Lacy Photography
www.aaronlacy.com

ISBN 978-0-9746231-4-6

JEREMY J. ANDERSON

POWER APPS

DAILY DOWNLOADED DEVOTIONALS
FOR YOUTH & YOUNG ADULTS

SPIRIT REIGN PUBLISHING
A Division of Spirit Reign Communications

ACKNOWLEDGEMENTS

To my wife, best friend, lover & supporter Traci, you are truly God sent. I am a better man because of you!

To my Father, Pastor Daryl S. Anderson Sr. Thank you for your tireless efforts in helping to get this project completed. Your work ethic and vision is Phenomenal.

To my editorial staff; Tawanna Anderson, Jan Ross, Erin Davis, Katie Arnette, Traci Anderson, Rita Gains, Twanna Collins & Jonae Jackson, thank you for your insight.

To my Family & Friends, thank you for your support and prayers.

To my Brothers on the "Prayer Line" just as iron sharpens iron, you all sharpen me.

To Pastor Roger R. Wade, and Pastor James L. Black Sr. Thank you for your encouragement and support.

DEDICATION

To my Heavenly Father, Provider, Counselor& Friend, thank you for your Unconditional Love, Indescribable Grace & Perfected plan for my life. I owe my life to you!

To all of my Young people in the world, this book is for you. Tap into the Power that God has for you so that you can fulfill your life's destiny.

CONTENTS

SECTION 3 YOUR POWER

SECTION 4 YOUR GROWTH

INTRODUCTION

When you think of the term "Power" you might think of; might, force, strength, potency, authority or energy. Do you ever wonder where your Spiritual power comes from? John 14:12 & 13 NLT says, "I tell you the truth, anyone who believes in me will do the same works I have done, and even greater works, because I am going to be with the Father. You can ask for anything in my name, and I will do it, so that the Son can bring glory to the Father." Here in this text, Jesus is telling His disciples that He gets His Power from God, and that when He is gone if we believe in Him we will have even more Power than He demonstrated here on Earth.

God has greatness for all of us and He is waiting to distribute it out. You have to ask yourself, are you ready to receive this power that Jesus talked about? "Power Apps" will give you a better understanding of God and His plan for your life. This book will also provide you with principles that you can practice daily to enhance your relationship with God and help you receive His Holy Spirit.

At the end of each day, you will find 3 tips that will help you fully understand the devotional and download your daily dose of Power. The first tip is the Power Passage, which is a bible text to read and take with you throughout the day. This text will reflect your devotional thought for the day. The second tip is the Power Point, which basically sums up the thought for the day in a clear and plain context. The third tip is the Power Prayer, which is a prayer for you to pray to

God seeking His Holy Spirit. This prayer will flow with the topic of the day. In addition to the Power Prayer, please add your own custom prayer to submit to our God above who love to answer your prayers. It is my prayer that throughout this book you will be enlightened, and encouraged to tap into the Power that God has for you!

SECTION 1 YOUR PURPOSE

DAY 1

THE CHOSEN 1

Congratulations! You have been selected in the cycle of life! Quite a bit was involved in order for you to be here today. For starters, your biological mother and biological father, at some point, got together and a miracle took place. You see, your father had approximately 500,000,000 sperms racing to penetrate and attach to your mother's one egg. You were made up of ½ of your mom's DNA and ½ of your father's DNA. It took 23 chromosomes from each of them to make one singular cell. That's where it all began for you. Interesting, yet true.

I feel pretty fortunate to be the young human being I am today. I have grown from one single cell to approximately 75 trillion cells. Every few seconds, thousands of your cells die and thousands more are being created. Isn't that amazing? What's really amazing is that you have a 3-billion character description in your DNA code. Psalm 139:13 says, "For you created my inmost being; you knit me together in my mother's womb." While you were in your mother's womb God was creating you!

Do you see what has happened? God chose you! Out of millions upon millions of sperms, "potential people," you were chosen. I use the term "chosen" because when you were swimming through your mom's fallopian tube you didn't know you were swimming. Don't you see? You didn't choose life, life chose you! Some tend to think we were born by chance or by accident. Galatians 1:15 NLT says, "But even before I was born, God chose me and called me by his marvelous grace." What does this mean? This text means you were not an accident. Even if you weren't a part of your biological parent's plan, you were a part of God's plan. You are here for a reason. You may not know now, but throughout this book you will begin to see God's power in your life.

You are a distinct and special individual, with all sorts of personality. There is not another person on planet Earth who is exactly like you. This means that there isn't anyone else on this Earth that can do what God has called you to do! You are more special to God than you know and He has a great plan for your life. All He asked for you to do is let Him lead and be #1 in your life. The first step to downloading the power that God has in store for you is to acknowledge that you were chosen and placed here for a reason.

Power Passage: "Before I formed you in the womb I knew you, before you were born I set you apart; I appointed you as a prophet to the nations." Jeremiah 1:5 NIV

Power Point: Many of us just exist, but to know Christ is truly living. You didn't choose life, life chose you. Jesus said in the Bible that He is the way, the truth and the LIFE. Choose Christ for he has already chosen you!

Power Prayer: Dear Father in Heaven, thank you for choosing and creating me. Help me to see and truly understand how much you love me and how special I am to you. Even though I don't fully see your plans for my life, give me the faith in you to trust you. You have placed me here for a reason, and I just ask that you will help me live out my purpose in life. When I feel low, weak and discouraged remind me that you have a plan for my life. Guard me from the enemy who only wants to discourage and destroy my life. Thank you for the fact that he cannot take my life, for you are the giver of life. Jesus, today I give you my life; have your way. Amen!

DAY 2

ROYALTY

What if I told you that you belonged to the royal family? Would you think I was talking about the royal family in England? What if I told you that you were a prince or princess? What If I told you that the GOD who created the Heavens and the Earth loved you so much that he designed and created you in his image? He created billions of other planets and galaxies, but He loved you so much that He created you in His image. Do you feel special? Well you should! Don't take my word for it, it's in the Bible. Genesis1:27 NLT says, "So God created human beings in his own image. In the image of God he created them; male and female he created them." So, if God is the King and Ruler of everything, what does that make you as His child? That's right, a prince or princess.

You are special to God and so precious, which is why you are such a threat to the enemy, Satan. Every time he looks upon the face of the human race he is reminded that we were created in the very image of the God that he wages war against. The devil has spent his entire career here on earth trying to deceive and destroy us, God's children. 1 Peter 5:8 NLT says, "Stay alert! Watch out for your great enemy, the devil. He prowls around like a roaring lion, looking for someone to devour." In these last days, our enemy will do all he can to stop us from fulfilling Gods purpose in our lives. He knows that he can be successful in your death if he can keep you from recognizing your worth. This is why we must come to the realization of our worth in Christ!

For years, the enemy told me that I wasn't worth anything. He told me that I would never get my life right. He even told me to stop trying to be a Christian because I would never be able to stop sinning. If the enemy was telling this to me then, I'm sure he is saying the same thing to you now. So let me say this...He is a liar! God's grace and mercy is bigger than your sin. Our so-called big sins have a way of making our God seem small. We actually think that our sins are so great that God can't free us from them.

If you are disconnected from God, sin has a way of making your God seem small, when in all actuality God has already taken care of your sins. The book of John says that if we confess our sins, then God will forgive us of them. Many times we lack true and sincere confession. Christ wants us to carry ourselves like we are a part of royalty. Let's practice some loyalty to the royalty. Satan's biggest trick is deception and discouragement, and if he can deceive or discourage you, then he feels he has the upper hand. This is when you go to the upper room and give God your discouragement, depression, confusion, frustration, doubt and anxiety, so that He can replace it with strength, courage, understanding and discernment.

Now that we have this out of the way, you're probably still asking yourself, "Why was I born or created?" The answer is simple; you were created to bring glory to God. Revelation 4:11 simply states that "all things were created for God's pleasure." He allowed you to be born so that He could love you and watch you grow up and live a beautiful life with Him. In your life, you should be bringing Him pleasure and making Him proud. I mean, we were created in His image. What an honor! You come from Royalty so honor God with your body and life, so that one day you can inherit your kingdom.

CLICK HERE TO DOWNLOAD

Power Passage: "But ye are a chosen generation, a royal priesthood, an holy nation, a peculiar people; that ye should shew forth the praises of him who hath called you out of darkness into his marvelous light." 1 Peter 2:9 KJV

Power Thought: You come from royalty, a holy dynasty, so be not afraid of the enemy! Regardless of what your earthly family is like, you have been chosen to be a part of God's family.

Power Prayer: God, thank you for creating me and for allowing me to be born. Help me to never doubt your love for me. Help me every day to make you proud while I fulfill my life's purpose. Show me what plans you have for me. Thank you for adopting me into your royal family. Help me to make you proud. At times I may not feel special, and when those times come, remind me how special I am to you. Guard me from the enemy so that I can be used by you! I love you, Amen!

JEREMY J. ANDERSON

DAY 3

GOD'S PLAN

I don't have any children, but I do have two nephews. Nickolas is 5 and AJ is 3. I love these little guys so much and want nothing but the best for them. At times I may seem a little stern with them, but it's only because I want what's best for their lives. Nothing gives me more joy than for them to ask me for something and see their faces light up when my answer is yes. Sometimes my answer is no, not because I don't want to do for them, but because Uncle Jeremy knows what's best. I've got some great things in store for these little guys when they get older. I guess you could say I have their whole life planned out in my head. I know what it takes to be successful in life and I can't wait to share it with them.

If my sister Ashley will allow me, of course, these guys will be playing organized sports, playing musical instruments and studying Kung-Fu. Okay; Tae-Kwon-Do. I want them to be advanced in many areas of life. By the time high school comes around I want them to be able to speak a foreign language and be on the honor roll (that way they can slide into any college at the top of their class). I will also teach them the value of having good credit and the importance of financial responsibilities. They will understand the value of a dollar and will be hard working, God-fearing men.

Once my wife, Traci, and I have children, we will have the same high goals for them. We will set our goals so high because we want the best for them. Just how I have high standards and a plan for my nephews, our God above has high standards and plans for our lives as well. Before we can really embrace our purpose in life we have to know and understand that God has a plan for our lives. God's only request is that we trust Him. Too often we try and take the lead in our own lives and that's where we fail. I must admit, for years I thought I knew what was best for my life. For years I did things my way and, time after time, I found myself falling flat on my face. I spent years questioning God only because I didn't understand His plan, nor did I want to follow it. Proverbs 3:5 NLT says, "Trust in the LORD with all your heart; do not depend on your own understanding, Seek his will in all you do, and he will show you which path to take."

This seems to be a pretty simple request, and it is. What makes this request at times challenging is when we get impatient with God. We must get to the point where we can, like the song says, "Let go and let God have His way." When we fall into sin, it's normally because we, as young people, want to do what we want to do. Often times, we're not concerned with what God wants in our lives, and when things fall apart, we cry out to Him to fix them. I get it, and so does God; we're stubborn and hard headed. When we reach the point where we follow Him regardless of what we want or think, we are on the path to reaching greatness.

CLICK HERE TO DOWNLOAD

Power Passage: "For I know the plans I have for you, declares the LORD, plans to prosper you and not to harm you, plans to give you hope and a future. Then shall ye call upon me, and ye shall go and pray unto me, and I will hearken unto you. And ye shall seek me, and find me, when ye shall search for me with all your heart." Jeremiah 29:11-13 NIV

Power Point: Beyond what you think, know that God has a plan for your life. This plan can only move forward if you are willing to submit your life to Him. This gives Him room to work. Allow Christ to be the Potter and you be the clay. The significant thing about clay is that once it's moist with water (Holy Spirit), it's able to be molded and shaped. Ask God to shape and mold you, so He can use you!

Power Prayer: Thank you, Lord, for having a plan over my life. Lord, please help me to be able to understand your plan, and even when I don't understand, help me to trust the process. Please fill me with your Holy Spirit so that you can shape and mold me to be what you want me to be. Take complete control of my life Jesus! Please forgive me of my sin, and help me so that my stubbornness doesn't delay your process. Thank you for trusting me with life, and help me to live it more abundantly through you! Amen!

JEREMY J. ANDERSON

DAY 4

INTERNAL FLAME

Have you ever wondered why you were born? What is your purpose? For years I asked myself, "Why am I here on Earth?" It's the question I get asked the most when I travel around the country talking to young people. It's in our human nature for us to question why we were born. When I was a little kid, I knew that I was sent here on earth to do super natural things. I just knew that one day I would get my calling and be like a super hero with super powers. You're probably laughing, but I was so very serious! I really and truly felt like there was something inside of me that was waiting to be ignited. There actually was! It's called my internal flame.

The first thing that was created was light. In Genesis, God simply said, "Let there be light," and there was light! God is so great that He can just think of something, and…BAM! There it is, in perfect form. I think it's interesting how the first thing that was created was light. I think that shows the true character of our God. Before life or anything else can be created, I must have light! In the Bible, light was meant to represent good, while darkness was meant to symbolize evil. There is no question that the world we live in today is full of sin and darkness. John 8:12 NLT says, "Jesus spoke to the people once more and said, "I am the light of the world. If you follow me, you won't have to walk in darkness, because you will have the light." This same light that Jesus is speaking of in John chapter 8 is the same light you have within you this very moment. The only question is, are you willing to turn that flame on?

Consider the idea that we are just like flashlights. A small flashlight has so much power because of what's inside of it. Now, the flashlight doesn't have any power until it is switched on. You could be in a huge dark house, or be totally lost in the woods, completely surrounded by darkness. But, no matter where you are, once you take out your flash light and cut it on, the light within will illuminate the area and cut through the darkness. The cool thing is that darkness cannot overpower light, but light can overpower darkness. If you're in a room filled with light, you can't cut darkness on, but if you're in a dark room, you can bring light to the room. This is the power that light has over darkness.

I remember speaking at a youth retreat. I was in the woods with about 12 other young people. We had a guide facilitating some activities, but we were soon lost in the darkness, trying to find our way back to the camp. No one really knew where to go, but once I switched the flashlight on, we were able to get back on track. Subsequently, everyone followed the light. I realized then the importance of light in a dark world. We are living in a dark, cold world where the majority of the people are lost. They are looking for something, but don't know what it is. By simply turning on your internal flame, people will naturally be drawn to you as well as follow you all the way to glory!

What good is power if we don't know how to use it? People will follow your internal flame as long as you share it. Don't be afraid to share the light that God has given you. In the woods that dark night, some of the guys in my group said they didn't need the light and knew where they were going, which got them more lost than they already were. Once I switched my flashlight on, they followed. You have an internal flame; the only question is, will you use it?

Power Passage: "You are the light of the world. A town built on a hill cannot be hidden. Neither do people light a lamp and put it under a bowl. Instead they put it on its stand, and it gives light to everyone in the house. In the same way, let your light shine before men, that they may see your good deeds and praise your Father in heaven." Matthew 5:14-16 NIV

Power Point: A fire that is out in the open will burn freely and shine brightly, but the fire that is closed in or bottled up will soon die. Be the light and fire that shines bright and warms up this cold world.

Power Prayer: God, please give me the courage to use my internal flame. Help me to let my light shine bright in this dark world. I know now that you have created me for your glory, so help me to shine bright for you. Please forgive me for my sins, and please take them away so they don't dim my light. At times while at school or work, it's hard to stand out, but please show me how to be a courageous Christian. We live in a dark world, so I ask that you will fill me with your Holy Spirit everyday so that I can let my light shine. Amen!

DAY 5

WHEN THE LIGHTS GO OUT

On April 28, 2011, the South was rocked with severe storms and dozens of tornadoes. The massive storm system killed at least 337 people across seven states. My state, Alabama, was hit extremely hard. We had many who lost their lives and hundreds of families who lost their homes. Whole schools and buildings were picked up and tossed around towns. Signs and large debris blew hundreds of miles away. I saw, with my own eyes, communities approximately two miles from my home completely destroyed.

Many counties, including the one I lived in, were without power for over a week. This was a tragic situation that placed everyone in survival mode. People were looting and stealing from the stores, seeking food and supplies. The prices for generators and other sources for electricity went through the roof. At the beginning of this crisis, everyone seemed to be looking out for themselves and their family. Many neighbors were not acting neighborly, and many communities had no sense of community.

We experienced something a little different where I lived. My neighborhood turned into a community, a community of people united. Right in my very cul-de-sac, we were given the opportunity to fellowship and hang out. My neighbors, who I only knew by waving at them as I drove by, were now people I had dinner with. Our whole community got together and barbecued nightly. I must admit, we had a really good time. The local news and radio stations soon reported that the same thing was happening across the state. Through this tragedy, people were united.

From this ordeal, I found out that many of my neighbors were Christians. We were put in a position that allowed us to testify of the goodness of the Lord and have some good Christian fellowship. Through this tragedy, God was glorified and we were able to unite as Christians and let our lights shine together. Churches and organizations around the state worked together for the same cause. During this time of disaster, we as Christians, were able to put aside our religion and focus on our relationships with one another. This world needs more relationships and true community.

A deep sense of awe came over them all, and the apostles performed many miraculous signs and wonders. And all the believers met together in one place and shared everything they had. They sold their property and possessions and shared the money with those in need. They worshiped together at the Temple each day, met in homes for the Lord's Supper, and shared their meals with great joy and generosity, all the while praising God and enjoying the goodwill of all the people. And each day the Lord added to their fellowship those who were being saved. Acts 2:43-47 NLT

Even here, in Acts, we witness a community coming together. This is what God has called us to do. Our society today molds us into being independent of other people; God wants us to unite as a people.

When the lights went out in my city, our internal lights came on. Boy was it bright! I could feel the positive energy around my city. People were glad to be alive and were eager to help one another. I saw the face of Jesus in many people during those times. Who knew that such a tragedy would be such a blessing? Sometimes that's what God has to do. During that time, God was telling us all to slow down and commune with one another. This is the power that we all have since we are followers and believers in Christ. Our internal flames are so powerful that they can unite communities, cities, states, countries, even the world. In order to demolish darkness, we must turn on the light.

CLICK HERE TO DOWNLOAD

Power Passage: "But everything exposed by the light becomes visible and everything that is illuminated becomes a light. This is why it is said: Wake up, sleeper, rise from the dead, and Christ will shine on you." Ephesians 5:13, 14 NIV

Power Point: Sometimes God will slow us down, so that we can lift Him up. Sometimes God has to turn off the lights of the world, so our internal flames can ignite and shine bright.

Power Prayer: God, please give me the power to show my true Christian stripes to the world. Help me to be so bold for you that I don't have to wait for something tragic to happen to witness to others. Give me Your Spirit, so when people see me; they see You! Give me the brightness and boldness of Your character so that people will be drawn to You! Please God fill me with Your Spirit so that I can be used by You. Amen!

DAY 6

IDENTITY CRISIS

The Bible says, in Genesis 1:27, that you and I were made in the image of God! There are billions and billions of galaxies, all filled with other planets, suns and stars. God loved us so much that He made us to look like Him! Even though we know this, if we don't know God then we may not have a specific identity. This can be challenging, especially for youth and young adults. Trying to fit in and be accepted by your classmates or coworkers creates a lot of pressure. This pressure can cause us to have an identity crisis.

For many years of my life, I dealt with an identity crisis. From high school, through college and even after college I went from one extreme to the next, searching for my identity. Who I was hanging out with determined my personality. If I needed to be, I was the class clown, bringing laughter to my peers while seeking their acceptance. In attempts to blend in with the educated crowd, I would adopt a sense of intellect to be accepted by my scholarly peers. At times, I hung around the so-called "pretty boys" who kept a fresh haircut and their clothes freshly pressed. I would also always have a hairbrush and cologne within reach. I'd like to think that this was the easiest culture for me to adapt to. Later in life, I would take on the role of a thug. I noticed how the girls seemed to like the bad guys, so I adopted that persona and, through many life-threatening experiences, pretended to be the bad guy. It became a way of life for me.

All in all, I was trying to find my inner true identity. Adults go through a mid-life crisis when they reach a certain age, but I was going through an identity crisis at a young age. Many of the personalities and cultures that I so freely adopted were nurtured and created by music, television and my surroundings. It wasn't until I matured that I truly realized I was a child of the King. I decided to show some loyalty to my royalty. Being loyal to my royal family made so much sense.

Some of you might know your parents and in them you may see a glimpse of yourself. On the other hand, some of you may not know your parents or, even if you do, you still may not see a glimpse of yourself in them. Whatever the case, you must get to a point when you look to Christ for that example. He is our ultimate example of the character we should want to emulate. He was loving, kind, patient, caring, understanding and compassionate. Being young in this world nowadays is rough, I know. There are so many pressures, distractions and temptations around every corner. It is important that you stay connected to Christ and that you keep your focus on Him.

Colossians 3:1-3 says, "Since, then, you have been raised with Christ, set your hearts on things above, where Christ is, seated at the right hand of God. Set your minds on things above, not on earthly things. For you died, and your life is now hidden in Christ in God. Stay focused on His power and plan for your life. Don't get mesmerized by the temporary things of this world. The devil's biggest trick is to make you feel as though you are an outcast to God's family and this is not true. No matter what you do God will be there with His arms out stretched waiting and willing to love you.

For most of my life, I tried to be accepted and I now know that God accepts me just how I am. My identity is now found in Christ.

Power Passage: "Therefore, as God's chosen people, holy and dearly loved, clothe yourselves with compassion, kindness, humility, gentleness and patience. Bear with each other and forgive one another if any of you has a grievance against someone. Forgive as the Lord forgave you. And over all these virtues put on love, which binds them all together in perfect unity. Let the peace of Christ rule in your hearts, since as members of one body you were called to peace. And be thankful. Let the message of Christ dwell among you richly as you teach and admonish one another with all wisdom through psalms, hymns, and songs from the Spirit, singing to God with gratitude in your hearts. And whatever you do, whether in word or deed, do it all in the name of the Lord Jesus, giving thanks to God the Father through him." Colossians 3: 12-17 NIV

Power Point: Someone once told me that God loves you just the way you are, and I believe that's true. But I also believe He loves you too much to leave you just the way you are. People tend to mimic what they see. In order for you to see Christ and take on His character, you have to spend more time with Him.

Power Prayer: Dear God, I need You! At times, this world can seem overwhelming and confusing. Give me clarity to know right from wrong, and then give me the strength to choose right over wrong. Help me to adopt Your character so that others can see You in me. Change my thinking and help me to have a deeper desire to spend time with You. Father, I also ask that every day I will get closer and closer to You. Please forgive me for my sins and thank You for Your grace and mercy. Help me to recognize my true identity in Christ Jesus, and then give me Your power so that I can embrace and proclaim it. Amen!

DAY 7

RUN YOUR ROUTE

I am a huge football fan. I like college football, but I love when the NFL season comes around. There are so many different elements to football—defense, offense, special teams, etc. You can score with a field goal, touchdown, or the 2-point conversion. Each team, I'm sure, would love to score touchdowns every time they have possession, but the reality is they won't. The defense in the NFL is composed with some of the biggest and toughest guys in the world. They get paid a lot of money to make sure the opposing team doesn't score. Not only do they not want you to score, but they are also trained to hit you, HARD! Imagine 300 lbs of power coming straight for you with only one intention, and that's stopping you!

My favorite position in football is the receiver. He's trained to run specific routes, patterns and plays because it puts him in a position to catch the ball. It's one of the most critical rules in football; the receiver must run his route. The opposing team has players specifically assigned to the receiver, and their job is to make sure the receiver doesn't catch the ball. The receiver must have faith and trust that his quarterback, the leader of the team, will get the ball to him. By running the route that was drawn up for him, the receiver is placing himself in a position to catch the ball.

There's nothing sweeter in the NFL than to see a receiver

run the route or play that was specifically drawn up for him and, as a result, catch the touchdown pass. There are a lot of talented players who play the game of football, but they don't want to run the route. Sometimes, receivers or running backs thinks that they are so good that they can do their own thing, only to look up in the sky and find disappointment when the ball isn't there, coming to them.

This scenario reminds me of my past life. I had so much victory in the past that I felt I could've lived my life here on earth successfully by running my own route. Countless times I would make it to the end zone of life, only to see the football I was supposed to catch go over my head. Other times, I would get knocked down "by the defender," the devil. If I had run the play that God drew up for me, I would've been in a position to receive my blessing from God. 1 Corinthians 15:58 NIV says, "Therefore, my dear brothers and sisters, stand firm. Let nothing move you. Always give yourselves fully to the work of the Lord, because you know that your labor in the Lord is not in vain." This scripture is encouraging you to be consistent in Christ. Don't let the opposition shake you up. Run your route and have faith that God will create an opening for you.

I'd like to imagine that God is the owner of the team, Jesus is the coach and the Holy Spirit is our all-time quarterback. God has given us a playbook, His Holy Bible. Just like the receiver, you must trust the route that God has drawn for you. Even when you feel the odds are stacked against you, run hard for Christ every time. Life will throw some big issues your way, but trust that God will make a way for you. Consistent faith in Christ is key. Like Donnie McClurkin says, "we fall down, but we get up!" That's how it is in football and in life. In order for us to be successful, we must study his playbook daily and run the routes so that we can be victorious in this game of life. At times, we might get knocked down but we have to keep fighting for righteousness. Are you ready to start scoring in your life? If so, success is just up the field, all you have to do is run the route!

Power Passage: "When David's time to die drew near, he commanded Solomon his son, saying, "I am about to go the way of all the earth. Be strong, and show yourself a man, and keep the charge of the LORD your God, walking in his ways and keeping his statutes, his commandments, his rules, and his testimonies, as it is written in the Law of Moses, that you may prosper in all that you do and wherever you turn." 1 Kings 2:1-3 NIV

Power Point: If the Lord didn't think you were good enough to play at a high level in life, He wouldn't put you in the game. You are here for a reason! Run the route and score for team Jesus!

Power Prayer: Lord, help me to get familiar with Your plays that You have given me in Your Bible. Help me to have a deeper desire to study Your word so that I can apply the steps in my daily life. When the enemy knocks me down, Lord, give me Your strength to get up and keep fighting. Please Lord, give me the faith in You and Your Word to follow Your plays. I also ask, Father, that every time I score in life, I be reminded to give You the praises. Shape and mold me, dear God, to be the receiver You want me to be. Amen!

SECTION 2 YOUR JOURNEY

DAY 8

UNDER CONSTRUCTION

I do quite a bit of traveling, speaking at different high schools. Every week, I'm on the road heading to a new school and often when I travel, I come across quite a bit of construction taking place. It seems that whenever I'm in a rush and I'm scheduled to get to the school just in time to prepare to speak, I come across construction zones. Construction zones, for most of us, seem to be an inconvenience. Although it's an inconvenience, it's always necessary. The construction that takes place on roads and highways is to make needed and necessary improvements to the conditions of the roads. Many times construction takes place simply to accommodate more drivers and provide a smoother and safer ride. Most of the improvements are to widen the roads, and sometimes transportation officials reduce a two-lane road to one lane so they can fix cracks and potholes.

What about construction work at your home? Now that I'm married, I find myself watching home improvement shows with my wife, Traci. I must say that some of the improvements that the contractors make to the homes are amazing. My favorite show is called "Extreme Makeover." The hosts of the show surprise a worthy family with a newly remodeled home. I have had some experience doing some home improvements myself. These improvements don't happen overnight and, depending on how bad the damage is and the improvements being made, the process can take a lot of time, effort and money. These home construction jobs are necessary when we remodel our homes. Sometimes we have to tear some walls down and pull up some old carpet, but once it's finished, the hard work, time and money pays off.

As we travel on this journey of life, we get comfortable on the route that we take. We get so comfortable that God may need to allow a little construction to take place within our own lives. Construction on what, might you ask? Construction on our character! Character flaws often result in pot holes, cracked roads, or a leaky ceiling. If we allow God to have His way in our lives, He will fix the cracks in our roads, which can stop us from getting to our final destination. Maybe there's a void or hole in your life that makes this ride called life bumpy and painful. God wants to fill those potholes to smooth out your trip. Maybe He just wants to knock some walls down in your life to make more room for Him to come in and abide in you?

As you are growing to become the person God has called you to be, you will come across some potholes in life. Luckily, God is the master rebuilder! He made you in the first place, so rest assured that He knows the best way to fix and improve you. This process will not always be convenient and, at times may be painful, but the Holy Spirit will keep you! Romans 5:3-5 NIV says, "Not only so, but we also glory in our sufferings, because we know that suffering produces perseverance; character; and character, hope. And hope does not put us to shame, because God's love has been poured out into our hearts through the Holy Spirit, who has been given to us." As we travel on this Christian journey, we, as Christians should be bringing others with us to meet Christ. Why is change or construction in our lives so necessary? Maybe God needs to widen our roads so we can have room to bring other people with us. Although the construction is not pretty and it seems like it's an inconvenience, it is mandatory for your growth. Let God change you, then let Him use you!

CLICK HERE TO DOWNLOAD

Power Passage: "Therefore, I urge you, brothers and sisters, in view of God's mercy, to offer your bodies as a living sacrifice, holy and pleasing to God—this is your true and proper worship. Do not conform to the pattern of this world, but be transformed by the renewing of your mind. Then you will be able to test and approve what God's will is—his good, pleasing and perfect will." Romans 12: 1-2 NIV

Power Point: You may find yourself in an area that looks like destruction, but it's really construction. Have faith in God to renovate your life! The construction that needs to take place in our lives will not always be fun and is sometimes painful, but it is equally necessary.

Power Prayer: Dear God, I know that I have flaws. Please forgive me of my sins! I give You this day complete control of my life. Please make the necessary changes to my life so that I can be used by You. Widen my roads and increase my territory so that I can reach more people. Break down the walls in my life that I have built up. Please Lord, fill every single room in my home with Your spirit and make me new each day. Help me to be the young person You have called me to be. Amen.

JEREMY J. ANDERSON

DAY 9

TRAFFIC SIGNS

Stop, Yield, Road Closed, Speed Limit, School Zone, Caution and One Way are just a few of the many traffic signs that you find on the roads and highways. They're put there for guidance throughout your journey. I must admit that the "One Way" sign has saved my life many times. One sign that I don't have too much respect for, but should, is the "No U-Turn" sign. Unfortunately, I still look left and right to make sure no cops are around before I do exactly what the sign has asked me not to do. Please pray for me, God's not done with me yet.

If you know how to follow a GPS and the traffic signs, then you should be able get to your destination with ease. I wish I could say the same for myself, I'm pretty hard headed. One day, I was traveling through a country town in west Alabama, on the way to visit one of my students. My GPS told me to go a different route than I was accustomed to going. Did I trust my GPS? Nope, I figured I was smarter than my GPS so I just continued on my normal route. A few miles from my student's house I noticed a sign that said, "Bridge CLOSED" and I thought to myself, "Yeah, right." I know what you're thinking, but I was really in denial this whole trip. I thought that maybe the county officials forgot to take the sign down.

As I got closer to the bridge, the signs got larger! What did I do? I slowed down, but still kept forward. As I approached the bridge, I saw that it was really closed. Go figure! At that moment, I didn't feel like the smartest person on the planet. To be completely honest, I actually got out of my truck to see if it was possible for me to make it across the bridge. I was determined to get across the bridge, but when I discovered the bridge was impassable, I reluctantly turned around. The sad thing about this situation was that I had all the warning signs. My GPS from the beginning told me not to go that route. When I ignored that, there were signs in place warning me of danger and telling me to turn around. Because of my reckless and stubborn behavior, I delayed my trip 40 minutes.

With no one to blame but myself, I asked God what lesson could be learned from this experience. He simply said to follow His lead, and stop leaning on our own knowledge. Sound familiar? Proverbs 3: 5-6 NLT says, "Trust in the LORD with all your heart; do not depend on your own understanding. Seek his will in all you do, and he will show you which path to take." How often do we question God's judgment? I had all the signs, but chose not to follow them. Do you sometimes find yourself disregarding the warning signs of life? If so, that's called disobedience. That's right, and if I learned anything from my days of being in the world, it's that disobedience causes delayed success. You will never accomplish what God has in store for you if you ignore His warning signs and guidance.

God has given us our own personal GPS (Gods Positioning System), which is His Holy Bible. It is the road map for success. It shows us how to handle and maneuver around every situation of life. The Bible even shows us where others went wrong, in hopes that we don't make the same mistake. God has also given us His Holy Spirit who is there to guide us every step of the way. You have two options—you can follow the plan and direction that God has for you, or you can be like me and delay your journey. My advice to you is to watch out for the closed bridge sign, and trust God's plan.

Power Passage: "Seek the LORD while he may be found; call on him while he is near. Let the wicked forsake their ways and the unrighteous their thoughts. Let them turn to the LORD, and he will have mercy on them, and to our God, for he will freely pardon. 'For my thoughts are not your thoughts, neither are your ways my ways' declares the LORD. "As the heavens are higher than the earth, so are my ways higher than your ways and my thoughts than your thoughts.'" Isaiah 55:6-9 NIV

Power Point: We will never understand God and His sovereignty. All we can do is trust the path that He has made for us.

Power Prayer: Dear God, thank You for the warning signs of life. Please help me to acknowledge the signs that You have placed around me. Remind me, oh Lord, not to lean on my own understanding, but help me to allow You to lead and guide me. Help me to spend more time in prayer and devotion to You so that I can clearly see the path that you have laid out for me. Forgive me for wondering off on my own, and thank You for always coming to rescue me. And, Father, please give me Your Holy Spirit, so that I will have the desire to follow Your path. Amen!

DAY 10

BUFFALO WINGS VS. AIRPLANE WINGS

Traci and I do quite a bit of traveling around the country speaking to the youth. Most of the time, we fly to our destination. Almost all of my trips go according to plan, except for this day. I was in route to speak at a church near Charlotte, NC and my layover was in the Baltimore, MD airport. Stepping off the plane, I knew that I had approximately 45 minutes before boarding would begin for my flight to Charlotte. My stomach whispered (grumbled) to me saying it was time for me to eat. Wow, I thought, I haven't eaten all day. I instantly went in search for the closest place that could satisfy my impatient taste buds. I soon found a nice restaurant two gates away from my soon-to-be departing flight.

Considering my flight time, I ordered a simple meal—Buffalo wings, French fries and a soda. My server was sweet, but my meal was even sweeter. I devoured the food; you would have thought I hadn't eaten the whole day. I guess that's my fault because I hadn't. After my meal, I asked my waitress for my check. In response, she offered me their strawberry cheesecake for dessert, then promised to have it right out for me. I declined and she asked was I sure and informed me of the whipped cream and fresh strawberries that come on top. I must admit, I fell for the option of whipped cream. This waitress must have had some magic power over me. I ordered the strawberry cheesecake and boy was it good.

Upon finishing the cheesecake, my waitress gave me the bill just as I was handing her my credit card. After leaving the restaurant, my belly was beyond full. I instantly regretted my strawberry cheesecake splurge. Walking through the terminal in route to where my plane was scheduled to depart from, I decided to purchase a few items that would assist me in my much needed nap on the plane. A magazine and one of those neck pillows that people wear on planes would be perfect, I thought. I stopped, made a few purchases and I was off.

When I got to my gate, I figured I was just in time because there was no line. I was greeted by a nice American Airlines attendant with a warm smile.

"You must be Mr. Anderson," she said.

"I am," I said.

"We've been expecting you."

I must admit, I felt pretty important! She then began to tell me about other flights she could put me on, either that night or the next morning, in order to reach my destination. I chuckled a bit and informed the young lady that I was scheduled to be on this flight. She chuckled back at me with that warm smile and informed me that I missed the flight and the gate had been closed. I smiled and said, "Well, open it." She smiled back and informed me of all the FAA rules and regulations and reasons why she couldn't open the gate for me.

"Are you telling me that I missed my flight?" I asked. "I'm afraid so, sir," she apologized. "I tried to wait on you. I even called your name several times on the intercom throughout the whole terminal."

Of course, I wasn't able to hear her because I was

enjoying my strawberry cheesecake. How silly did I feel? Thank God she was able to get me on the first flight out in the morning, which would put me in Charlotte, NC in time to get to my hotel and make it to church by 10:30am.

Before searching for a hotel to spend the night, I sat there at the terminal to reflect on what just happened. I believe that there is a lesson in everything in life, so I asked God what was the lesson to learn from this experience. He softly whispered to me that I symbolize the average Christian, my soon departing flight symbolized the second coming and that my hunger for the food more than my flight symbolized our desire for worldly things over being prepared for our journey home!

WOW! How true is that? We know that Christ's return is soon, but our focus and attention isn't there. God tells us in John 14: 2 & 3 that "There is more than enough room in my Father's home. If this were not so, would I have told you that I am going to prepare a place for you? When everything is ready, I will come and get you, so that you will always be with me where I am." All we have to do to claim this promise is believe in Him and be prepared when He comes. The problem is that, at times, we spend our time focusing on the pleasures of life.

My focus should have been sitting next to airplane wings, but instead, I was focused on my Buffalo wings. As opposed to catching my flight to spiritually feed the awaiting congregation, I was more concerned with feeding my belly. The same way the American Airlines attendant repeatedly called my name over the intercom, so does Christ call our names in order to warn us of His second coming. Revelations 3:20 NIV says, "Here I am! I stand at the door and knock. If anyone hears my voice and opens the door, I will come in and eat with him, and he with me." I was unable to hear the attendant call my name because I was outside of the terminal. Some of us are living outside of God's will and are on the verge of missing the flight of our lives. We are not where we should be because our desires and priorities are not where they should be. It's time for us to get our priorities straight. Is there anything worth missing out on eternity with Christ?

Power Passage: "But about that day or hour no one knows, not even the angels in heaven, nor the Son, but only the Father. As it was in the days of Noah, so it will be at the coming of the Son of Man. For in the days before the flood, people were eating and drinking, marrying and giving in marriage, up to the day Noah entered the ark; and they knew nothing about what would happen until the flood came and took them all away. That is how it will be at the coming of the Son of Man." Matthew 24: 36-39 NIV

Power Point: Ask yourself what's important to you. Then ask yourself if that's a priority. What's important isn't always a priority. We must make sure that the things that truly matter in life are a priority in life. These things of the world will soon pass away. The question is will you pass away with it, or will you claim the riches God has in store for you?

Power Prayer: Heavenly Father, I know that You have prepared a place for me in Heaven. Help me to stay focused on You so that one day I can claim my prize. Help me to stay focused on Your plan for my life, while avoiding the temptations of the world. I don't want to miss out on heaven so please give me Your Holy Spirit so that I can clearly hear Your voice when you call me. Thank You, God, for not giving up on me and for Your patience. I love You. Amen!

POWER APPS

DAY 11

GOOD FRIENDS

Here's a question for you, how many friends do you have? Better yet, do you consider yourself a friend to others? Now I don't mean acquaintances, or people who you hang out with from time to time. I'm talking about true friends. I've had the pleasure to be blessed with really good friends. Because I have an outgoing personality, I naturally make friends, but those aren't close friends. I have some close friends that will back me up regardless of the situation. I can call on them at any time of the night, and if physically possible, they will be there.

Childhood friendships are great. Having close friends throughout middle school, high school and college is great also, but having true spiritual friends is even greater. Spiritual friends, who care and nurture your growth in Christ, are God sent. It is imperative in your Christian journey to travel with other soldiers for Christ who, spiritually speaking, want to go the same place as you.

I mentored a young man who was having a really hard time growing spiritually after he was baptized. All of his friends still went to night clubs, did drugs and basically lived his "old" lifestyle. He would tell me how hard it was to stand for God when his surroundings only wanted to pull him down. I simply told him that he needed to place himself in a position to be spiritually successful. I did not tell him to disown his friends, for that's not what Christians should do.

He just needed to be mindful of the places they spend time together.

I once heard the true story of a man in the 1900's who traveled through a horrible snowstorm. He left his village to deliver medical supplies to the next town, 30 miles away. With only 5 miles left in his journey, the winter storm began to get the best of him. His walking slowed until he couldn't take another step. The traveler laid himself in the snow and looked up as his last few breaths whisked away into the cold, dark night. His hands began to turn pale as his eyes closed, accepting what was about to happen. Just then, the traveler heard a moan! He thought that it was just his imagination, until the moan got louder. He gathered the strength to sit up and listen for the sound. He heard the moan again! He stood up, took a step and began searching for, what sounded like, another person in distress. His heart began to beat faster and faster as he got closer to the moaning. It was another traveler who got lost and gave up on his way to the village! He helped the man up and, together, they found the strength to finish their journey.

Make sure you aren't traveling alone on your spiritual journey. Revelation 12: 11 NIV says, "They triumphed over him by the blood of the Lamb and by the word of their testimony." That means we will be victorious because we've been washed in the blood of Jesus and because we've relied on each other for support, for encouragement. You must understand the importance of having real spiritual friends that will assist you on this journey. And remember, friendship is a two-way street. You should be giving and receiving prayers and encouragement.

There are no real renegade Christian soldiers. Even Jesus wasn't alone; He had a crew of friends. Twelve disciples followed him everywhere he went. The disciples were companions that Jesus chose personally. He chose fishermen, a tax collector, a twin, and others. They traveled with Jesus as He preached, and once He died, they traveled and told others of Him. Throughout Christ's ministry here on earth, he had those who traveled along this journey with Him.

Jesus knew the importance of having spiritual friends. When the disciples went out to preach Jesus sent them out in groups of two because He knew of the value of spiritual backup! Mark 6:7 NIV says, "Calling the Twelve to him, he sent them out two by two and gave them authority over evil spirits." On this journey, the enemy will try to put you in a corner and beat up on you. Satan is a coward and bully, and knows that he has power as long as he can keep you silent. Now is the time to surround yourself with people who will be supportive of your walk with Christ. Who is your spiritual backup?

CLICK HERE TO DOWNLOAD

Power Passage: "Again I say to you, if two of you agree on earth about anything they ask, it will be done for them by my Father in heaven. For where two or three are gathered in my name, there am I among them." Matthew 18:19-20 ESV

Power Point: An accountability partner is vital in your Christian walk! The Bible says that iron sharpens iron, just how men should sharpen each other. Who do you sharpen? Who sharpens you?

Power Prayer: God, thank you for the gift of friendship. You know the people in my life right now, and I ask that you will protect me from the relationships that are harmful to my spiritual growth. Please Lord, place more people in my path that will be nurturing to my walk with You. Also Lord, please give me the power to be a good friend to others and I pray that I will have true love for them and concern for their growth as well. Thank you, Lord, for calling me Your friend. Amen!

JEREMY J. ANDERSON

DAY 12

BEST FRIENDS FOREVER

Let's be honest with ourselves. Life will not always be perfect and sweet. There will be times when you won't be able to call a friend. Or maybe you can call a friend, but you won't have the strength to pick up the phone. I have had some depressing lows in my life. I've been to the point where I didn't want to talk or be around anyone. Whatever you're feeling or going through, there is One who will always be in your corner.

The enemy wants to keep you isolated. That's when the devil works best. He wants you to keep your pain and suffering to yourself so that he can be free to mentally torture you. There have been times in my life when I felt so low and alone that I didn't want to turn to anyone. I could have picked up the phone and cried out to my parents or to some friends but sometimes I just wanted to be alone.

The good news about being alone is that it's actually impossible. We know about God the Father and God the Son, but what about God the Spirit? In the book of John chapter 14, Jesus called the Spirit many names. Depending on the translation, the Spirit of God is called Comforter, Counselor, Helper or Advocate.

"And I will ask the Father, and he will give you another advocate to help you and be with you forever—the Spirit of truth. The world cannot accept him, because it neither sees him nor knows him. But you know him, for he lives with you and will be in you." John 14:16&17 NIV In these two verses, Christ is telling His disciple that He will be sending them the Holy Spirit. The Spirit of God is there to hold you when you're lonely, to be a blanket when you're cold, to keep you when you're lost, to give guidance when you need direction, to give you strength when you are weak, to be the light in the darkness, to be your voice when you have no words and to pick you up when you are down.

You know that guilty conscience that speaks to you when you're doing wrong? That's the Holy Spirit! That sense of courage after you pray? That's the Holy Spirit! You have a friend above all friends. How does it feel to have someone that will always be there regardless of how we treat Him?

I think that one of the biggest misconceptions about our Friend, the Holy Spirit, is that He will treat us like we treat our friends. If you go a week or so and don't talk to a friend, things may seem weird for a bit. Maybe one of you will have an attitude and then, after a while, things will return to normal. It's not like that with God. He doesn't hold grudges if you haven't talked to Him in a while. He is patiently waiting there for you to accept Him. This is what you call a true "Best Friend Forever" because He isn't going anywhere. As a matter of fact, if you choose, you can spend eternity with Him!

CLICK HERE TO DOWNLOAD

Power Passage: "Do not be anxious about anything, but in every situation, by prayer and petition, with thanksgiving, present your requests to God. And the peace of God, which transcends all understanding, will guard your hearts and your minds in Christ Jesus. Finally, brothers and sisters, whatever is true, whatever is noble, whatever is right, whatever is pure, whatever is lovely, whatever is admirable—if anything is excellent or praiseworthy—think about such things. Whatever you have learned or received or heard from me, or seen in me—put it into practice. And the God of peace will be with you." Philippians 4: 6-9 NIV

Power Point: Always remember, when you reach your lowest low or your highest high, the Holy Spirit will be there and He is the ultimate comforter. This is the same Holy Spirit who will be there to give you spiritual power upon request. I don't know of anyone or thing that will always be there for you 24/7. Take advantage of the Spirit for therein lies your power!

Power Prayer: Father in Heaven, thank You so much for the gift of the Holy Spirit. Thank You for always being there for me. Please help me to lean on Your Spirit more often, and help me to take complete advantage of Your power so that I can share it with others. Fill me up today with the power of Your Holy Spirit, so that I will be able to handle whatever the day brings my way. Amen!

JEREMY J. ANDERSON

DAY 13

GOOD HAIR

The hair on your head is very interesting. Often times our hair accentuates our outer image. We all have different types of hair—short, long, curly, straight, blonde, black or brunette. Some wear it up, and some wear it down. Some braid it, and some put it in a ponytail. Some of you may even shave your head bald daily, like I do.

One day while in my bathroom, I noticed the shampoo and conditioner my wife uses on her hair. I read the back of the bottles. Shampoo helps to untangle your hair, clean the scalp, and roots of your hair. Then I found out that you use the conditioner after you clean your hair with the shampoo. The job of the conditioner is to help the hair keep its fresh, clean look, while giving it more bounce and shine. The conditioner also helps to seal nutrients into the hair. If you use these often, the shampoo and conditioner bottles promise to help your hair grow healthier and longer.

Later that day, my wife came home from her hair salon appointment, and I noticed that her hair was a little shorter. I knew that Traci wanted longer hair so I couldn't understand why she would allow her hairdresser to cut it. I asked her about it and she said that in order for your hair to grow you have to cut off your split ends. Not quite understanding, I asked my wife to clarify. Traci then began to explain that to keep her hair growing healthily, she not only needed to wash it, using shampoo & conditioner, but she also had to cut off the damaged parts of her hair that had stopped her hair from growing to its fullest potential. She had to get rid of the split ends.

I look at how our hair grows and realize now that there are specific things that must be done so that it grows healthy and strong. I can't help but think about us as Christians. How do we in our spiritual lives grow like beautiful long strands of hair? Below are some lessons I learned from my Hair 101 class with Traci.

Lesson 1: Just how shampoo cleans the hair and scalp, we need Christ daily to cleanse us from the sins that keep us down, to heal our damaged lives and clean us down to the root.

Lesson 2: Just as the conditioner is used to seal and protect the hair after it's cleaned, we need the Holy Spirit to dwell within us, seal us up, and add more bounce and shine to our lives.

Lesson 3: Just how you have to cut the unhealthy split ends from your hair, we, as growing, powerful Christians, must learn to cut some relationships from our lives. Some of us have some damaging people connected to us, and this is stopping us from growing spiritually.

The same way you need shampoo, conditioner, and your split ends trimmed to have healthy, growing hair, you must apply the same concept to have a healthy, growing spiritual life. Ask Christ daily to come into your life and wash your sins away. Then ask for the power of the Holy Spirit to fill you, seal you while you make the necessary changes in your life, and remove the things that's stopping you from growing.

CLICK HERE TO DOWNLOAD

Power Passage: "Assuming that you have heard about him and were taught in him, as the truth is in Jesus, to put off your old self, which belongs to your former manner of life and is corrupt through deceitful desires, and to be renewed in the spirit of your minds, and to put on the new self, created after the likeness of God in true righteousness and holiness." Ephesians 4:21-24 ESV

Power Point: The growth that takes place on the inside will soon show on the outside. You must be renewed daily by the Holy Spirit and be created anew. Everyday more of your old self should die off.

Power Prayer: Father in Heaven, please help me to recognize that I need You and Your Holy Spirit daily. Also, reveal to me the split ends in my life that need to be cut. If I am not strong enough to cut my personal split ends, then please cut them for me. Wash me with the blood that You shed for me on Calvary, seal me with Your Holy Spirit and talk with me throughout the day. Amen!

DAY 14

BABES IN CHRIST

Remember how simple life was when you were a baby? Probably not. I don't remember how life was when I was a baby either, but I get an idea from the lifestyle I see other babies live! Babies usually have someone taking great care of them. Why?Because they're babies. While in Atlanta waiting on a flight, I decided to visit friends who lived less than 10 minutes from the airport. While sitting in my friend's living room, I noticed a small TV on the floor next to their big TV. I asked my friend about the small TV he was watching and he told me it was a baby monitor. He then explained to me that he has a camera in his 2-year-old son's bedroom so he can watch his every move.

I sat there in amazement, wishing I had though up the idea of using cameras in a baby's room. I was more entertained by the baby monitor than the TV! The baby began tossing and turning like he was about to wake up. Realizing what was about to happen, my friend immediately excused himself from the room to grab his son. As my friend raced through the living room headed for the stairs, the baby did something very interesting. When he woke up, he looked around and when he didn't see his father there, he let out a load, singular cry-scream. I say "cry-scream" because that's just what it was! Just a loud and aggressive "WAAAA!" followed by a peaceful pause of silence. The baby then looked left and right again, expecting his father to magically appear. When he didn't show up in that instant, he went into a full sail, crying session. I mean the kicking and screaming kind. *"Gosh, little guy, daddy's on the way,"* I thought. Seconds later, I saw my friend jump in like superman and grabbed the baby out of the crib that held him against his will. He wrapped his son in his arms and whispered, "Calm down, daddy's here, it's OK."

As soon as my friend saw his son was awake, he immediately went to get him. As soon as the baby saw that his daddy wasn't there, he threw a temper tantrum. Both parties recognized that there was a need. The father recognized that the baby wanted out the crib, so he made his way there. The baby wanted out of the crib, but since he couldn't see his father working to make his way there, he cried. The father knew what the baby wanted even before the baby did.

Now, let's look at our lives. As we go through our Christian walk we are just like this baby. We all have things that we need or want, but as soon as God doesn't show up when we think He should, we begin to question His love for us. In all actuality, God knows what we want and need even before we do. God isn't held within the realms of time. He is omnipresent and all-knowing. We serve a sovereign God, and He's bigger than any situation. Whatever the need, we have the luxury of casting all of our cares on the Lord!

As you go throughout this Christian journey, you will have many struggles. You must know and believe that God is in control of everything. Let's not be anxious like the baby in this story, but let us be cool, calm and collected knowing that our Savior is on the way. Philippians 4:6 NIV says, "Do not be anxious about anything, but in everything, by prayer and petition, with thanksgiving, present your requests to God." As we grow in Christ, we will become more mature. We all have those baby moments when we pout and whine, but as we grow and we get more mature spiritually, we will have the faith that God is in control. Having true faith in God is a struggle for many of us, but practice makes perfect. Practice your faith!

Power Passage: "Ask and it will be given to you; seek and you will find; knock and the door will be opened to you. For everyone who asks receives; the one who seeks finds; and to the one who knocks, the door will be opened." Matthew 7:7&8 NIV

Power Point: God knows every single thing that you want. Have faith in Him and His promises. When Solomon became king, God asked him what he wanted. The only thing that Solomon asked for was wisdom so that he could be a good ruler. Because Solomon's heart was in the right place, God blessed him with wisdom and riches. Make sure your heart is in the right place when praying to God and have faith that He will answer your prayers.

Power Prayer: Dear God, thank You for being available to listen to my prayers, and thank You for answering my prayers. Thank You for the prayers that You answered "no," for You know what's best for me. You have been there for me every time I have needed You and I thank You for it. Please give me Your Spirit so that I can know what to ask for when I pray. Also, please give me Your patience when things don't come when I expect them and help me to practice my faith in You. Amen!

DAY 15

THE UNDERDOGS

I love the underdogs of life, especially in sports. If I'm not a fan of either team playing the game, whether it's basketball, baseball, or football, I root for the underdog. The underdogs are those that are thought to have little chance of winning a fight, contest, competition, or game. Some of the greatest stories in life are those when the underdog fights back to win in the end. The interesting thing about underdogs is, normally, no one believes in them, except for themselves. I think believing in yourself is key. As the saying goes, if you don't believe in yourself, then no one else will either.

I was an underdog. Because of my behavior, my 8th grade teacher told me I wasn't "high school material." Who says that to a middle school student? The teacher didn't even allow me to participate in my graduation services. When I got to high school, I started off proving the teacher right. After a few years, God brought teachers into my life who truly cared for me and this is what fueled me to be successful in life. I began to apply myself and after graduating from high school I went to college, and after college, I went on to graduate school. Through it all, God kept me and smiled on my life. He had a plan for me, even though some people may have not believed in me.

I can't help but notice some of the plans God had for His children found in the Bible. One of my favorite stories is David vs. Goliath. Goliath, the champion warrior of the Philistines, stood almost 10 feet tall. His armor alone weighed

125 lbs. David, a young shepherd boy, answered the call that no one else would. David had courage and confidence in his God, and that was all he needed for battle. The story is only as powerful as David's faith in God.

In Daniel, chapter 6, we see Daniel was sent to the lion's den. Those who set him up were probably snickering. The king didn't want to throw Daniel in prison but he felt like he had no choice, due to the law he made. I'm sure everyone around the palace thought that Daniel was sure to get eaten by the lions. Even the king was hoping that Daniel's God would deliver him from the mouth and hunger of the lions. God kept the lion's mouth shut because of Daniel's faith and commitment to God and His law. When everyone thought that Daniel was done, God was just getting started.

Joseph was kidnapped by his own brothers, thrown into a pit, and sold into slavery. The Bible says that "God was with Joseph." In spite of Joseph's circumstances, he remained faithful to God. Even when Joseph refused to fall to the temptations of Potiphar's wife and was thrown into prison, he still remained faithful to God. After years of being in prison, Joseph's faithfulness to God paid off. Joseph became second in command in all of Egypt. Joseph went from the pit, to Potiphar's house, to prison, then to the palace! If that's not an underdog success story, then I don't know what is.

What about you? Do you sometimes feel like your back is against the wall or you're all by yourself? Do you feel like an underdog? If you do, know that there is hope for you. God says in Romans 8:31, "What shall we then say to these things? If God be for us, who can be against us?" Think of Romans 8:31 when you are faced with adversity and know that you will always be victorious through Jesus Christ!

CLICK HERE TO DOWNLOAD

Power Passage: Exodus 14:14 NIV "The LORD will fight for you; you need only to be still." Ephesians 2:8-10 NIV "For by grace you have been saved through faith. And this is not your own doing; it is the gift of God, not a result of works, so that no one may boast. For we are his workmanship, created in Christ Jesus for good works, which God prepared beforehand, that we should walk in them."

Power Point: During moments when the impossible is evident, God shows up and proves that all things are possible through Him. Your condition doesn't have to be your conclusion. Keep pushing and allow God to fuel your success!

Power Prayer: Dear God, thank You for fighting for the underdogs. Help me to have complete faith in You to fight all of my battles. Place me where You want me to be and help me to trust Your judgment when things get rough. Thank You for never giving me more than I can handle, and thank You for providing a way out for me in rough situations. Please give me Your power so that the only thing I fear is You. Father, please give me the courage of David and the faith of Joseph so that I can be used by You. Amen!

SECTION 3 YOUR POWER

DAY 16

JAILBREAK
PART 1

Cell phones are so cool! Not only are they cool, but they are also convenient. Everything from Apple, Samsung, and Motorola, to HTC, Nokia, and LG are just some of the cell phone manufacturers that are taking the world by storm. It seems that every time you turn on the TV, you see a cell phone commercial. The market for cell phones is big because of the technology that it uses. Cell phones do more than just make and receive calls. For many of us, they replace our work calendar, alarm clock, computer, watch, digital camera, GPS, radio, MP3 player, and even our Bible! My iPhone does everything, except cook dinner for me! I must admit that, although I am not "techy," I still love a good device that can handle all of my technical needs.

As cool and advanced as our cell phones are, they are still very limited. After preaching at a church in Chattanooga, I met two young teenage guys who were computer whizzes. Over lunch after the service ended, these two young brothers, ages 17 and 19 began telling me they knew how to jailbreak computers and cell phones. Now, I'd heard of jailbreaking a phone before, but never had I actually met someone who could unlock or jailbreak one. I was intrigued, and honestly, doubted their skills, so I began to question them on how the process worked.

In an attempt to prove to me that they knew what they

were talking about, they began to break down the process and give clear descriptions on how to do it. They also explained that jailbreaking a cell phone allows you to tap into unlimited possibilities. By jailbreaking the phone, you remove limitations, gain root access to the operating system and unlimited powers and features. In addition to all of this, you also have no roaming charges! Then, my new computer whiz friends told me that in order to jailbreak a phone you have to get connected to your device's true source, like a Mac or a PC. The maker, or "creator," of your specific cell phone device created it so that it would be able to do all sorts of amazing things. Once the phone is made, there are programs in place to block certain privileges. These restrictions are made to keep users from accessing technology that hasn't been released yet.

This reminds me of our lives. God has created us in His image. We were beautifully and wonderfully made to do some amazing things for Him. The powers that we have when we are connected with God are incredible, but like the modern cell phones some of us are locked. Little do we know, we are programmed. That's right, we are programmed. Programmed to doubt God, programmed to lust, programmed to be greedy, and programmed to think church is boring.

In order for you to "jailbreak yourself" and grow spiritually, you must, just like a cell phone, be connected to the "Source." One way to connect yourself to the Source is to always put things that are spiritually healthy in your life. Philippians 4:8 NLT says, "And now, dear brothers and sisters, one final thing. Fix your thoughts on what is true, and honorable, and right, and pure, and lovely, and admirable. Think about things that are excellent and worthy of praise."

God tells us to focus on good things because He knows it can disconnect us from the Source. Essentially, what you see and hear will affect your heart and mind.

Every time you watch one of those new reality shows on TV or listen to your favorite secular artist, and you find yourself wishing you had their lifestyle, you're being programmed and disconnecting little by little from the Source. Next time you're looking at your favorite program, ask yourself, "What type of message is this putting in my mind?" When you hear your favorite song on the radio, ask yourself, "What type of feeling am I getting from that song?" If we can distance ourselves from things that prohibit us from growing spiritually, we can remove our limitations, gain root access to God's power, and unlock our lives so that we can reach our true potential.

CLICK HERE TO DOWNLOAD

Power Passage: "To the Jews who had believed him, Jesus said, 'If you hold to my teaching, you are really my disciples. Then you will know the truth, and the truth will set you free.' They answered him, 'We are Abraham's descendants and have never been slaves of anyone. How can you say that we shall be set free?' Jesus replied, 'Very truly I tell you, everyone who sins is a slave to sin. Now a slave has no permanent place in the family, but a son belongs to it forever. So if the Son sets you free, you will be free indeed. I know that you are Abraham's descendants. Yet you are looking for a way to kill me, because you have no room for my word.'" John 8:31-37 NIV

Power Point: You will never reach the success that God has planned for your life until you allow His Holy Spirit to come into your life. You must guard your ears, eyes, and mouth because it will affect your righteous mind.

Power Prayer: Heavenly Father, thank You for the gift of choice. Please help me to choose to love You every day, and show me how to love You. Make me aware of the things in my life that block me from you, and will be harmful to my spiritual growth. Please fill me up with Your Holy Spirit so that I can change some of the negative things that I'm so accustomed to doing. Have Your way within my life and change my thinking so that I can see You more clearly. Amen!

DAY 17

JAILBREAK
PART 2

Yesterday we discovered the term "jailbreak" means to tap into something's (or someone's) true source of power to unlock its raw potential. Many argue that there's nothing wrong with jailbreaking a cell phone and that if the creator of the phone didn't want you to have certain rights and privileges, he wouldn't have made the phone capable to do those things. Others will argue that it is definitely wrong to jailbreak phones and you should follow the plan of the programmers. You know, just go with the flow like everyone else in society.

Some people will tell you to just be "normal" in life and follow the ways of the world. They will tell you to follow the crowd and to do what everyone else is doing. They will reassure you and tell you that it's cool and that everyone does it. Most will take the latest fashion that they see on TV and make that the theme of their wardrobe. Others will follow music artist and emulate them. Most people will do exactly what they are programmed to do. Will you be able to stand and jailbreak your mind from the captivity of the modern day programming? Will you be bold enough to stand for Christ even when it doesn't seem like the cool thing to do? If the answer is yes, then you must be prepared for society to turn its back on you.

I remember being in the Apple store after my encounter

with my computer whizzes. I overheard a guy at the counter trying to get his phone fixed, but the only problem was that he jailbroke his phone. The Apple employee turned his nose up and said that since he violated the terms of agreement then his phone was no longer under warranty.

Once you step outside the box and decide to give your life to Christ and live solely for him, those of the world will turn their backs on you. Be prepared to lose some friends or your job. Maybe your neighbors will isolate you, or co-workers will start acting weird, but whatever it may be, just be prepared because the world doesn't follow Jesus. The world clearly puts its focus on money, fame, fashion, and wealth.

Be prepared for persecution. That's right, the same way the world persecuted Christ, some of us, His followers, will endure some persecution. 2 Timothy says this, "You, however, know all about my teaching, my way of life, my purpose, faith, patience, love, endurance, persecutions, sufferings—what kinds of things happened to me in Antioch, Iconium and Lystra, the persecutions I endured. Yet the Lord rescued me from all of them. In fact, everyone who wants to live a godly life in Christ Jesus will be persecuted." Not all persecution is deadly. Some may be at your home, community, or on your job. People may talk about you and treat you mean, but know that what Christ endured was far worse. Just know that true Christianity is not the most popular way of life these days. There are a lot of us who claim to follow Christ but won't carry our cross.

By breaking free from the "programming" of the world, you are able to see God clearly. Your whole life doesn't revolve around planet Earth. Your mind and life isn't centered and restricted to what this round mass of land and water has to offer, for you know of a place that is far greater than we can imagine. A place that is designed just for you! So the next time a rock star says, "This is the life," just smile and remind yourself of the promises that God gives in John 14:3 NIV "And if I go to prepare a place for you, I will come back and take you to be with me that you also may be where I am." He gave His life for you; will you give yours for Him?

CLICK HERE TO DOWNLOAD

Power Passage: "I have given them your word. And the world hates them because they do not belong to the world, just as I do not belong to the world. I'm not asking you to take them out of the world, but to keep them safe from the evil one. They do not belong to this world any more than I do. Make them holy by your truth; teach them your word, which is truth. Just as you sent me into the world, I am sending them into the world." John 17:14-18 NLT

Power Point: By breaking free from the mental and spiritual captivity of the world, you place your life in the position to do even greater things for God. The depth of God's love for you is what helped Him get through those times of persecution. Unless you truly love God you will be unable to stand for Him during rough times.

Power Prayer: Dear God, thank You for dying for my sins. Thank You for allowing yourself to be tortured, beat, stripped naked and hung for my sins. Thank You for loving me so much that You gave your sinless life for my sins. Help me, dear God, to love You that way. Help me to be strong and established in Your word. Give me Your Spirit and power to weather whatever storm You allow to come my way. Through all my experiences, God, I pray that it builds my faith in You. Fill me with Your Spirit this day Lord. Amen!

DAY 18

GOD CLOUD

Ok, so you have probably noticed by now that I love technology. My wife, Traci, and I needed a new computer. We decided to look into getting a Macbook Pro. This is a pretty interesting device. The Macbook is different from a regular PC. Its capabilities and features are greater than the average PC, from its design, software, and casing, to its battery life, and ability to multi-task. The sad thing about the Macbook Pro is that even after all that research, I really haven't tapped into all it has to offer. I learn something new every day.

Before I settled on purchasing a Macbook, I decided to go by the Apple store and test it out. I asked the technicians questions about their services and products. I must admit that I am not a tech-savvy person. I still have caveman tendencies when it comes to electronic devices, but I'm getting better. After drilling them with the best questions I could think of, I was convinced that the Macbook Pro was worth the investment.

One thing that helped me make the decision to invest in a Macbook was the "iCloud." The iCloud is a system that syncs all of your Apple devices and, at the same time, stores and saves your data. It's like a huge operating system in the clouds that stores your calendars, contacts, emails, books, music, documents, photos, etc. Once you save your stuff or upload data to your iPhone or iPad, it automatically goes up into the iCloud. Then, when you need those documents, you can reach up to this invisible technical cloud, wirelessly pull down what you need, and load it onto any of your Apple devices.

Needless to say, I was impressed with this service and operating system. After further reflection, I began to think about what they offer and it reminded me of something my Heavenly Father does. You see, like Apple devices, we have different aspects of our lives; we are sons and daughters, we have school, homes, work and social life to worry about. God is high above our earthly clouds and satellites just waiting to store our every prayer and concern. His Word says in 1 Peter 5:7, "Give all your worries and cares to God, for he cares about you." Your deepest desire, your every thought, your concerns and request, God says, "Give them to Me!"

The iCloud stores your information for your electronic devices and sends the stuff down as requested. Our God does so much more! Before we can even pray for things, He already knows. Don't take my word for it; read Matthew 6:8 NLT! It says, "… your Father knows exactly what you need even before you ask him!" Are you impressed yet? Apple doesn't even compare to our God! His word says that He knows what we need before we can even request it. Once we throw up our prayers to God, He stores those prayers. Then, when the time is right, He sends down the answer to our prayer, or the blessings we're waiting for.

As impressive as the iCloud seems, when I look up in the blue sky and see real clouds that my God created, I can't help but smile. He created those clouds to be more than shade from the sun, but to also be a pathway for our prayers. I know that He is beyond the clouds catching every prayer, every tear, every concern and He acts accordingly. When you think about how great God is, the iCloud doesn't seem so impressive. God has been doing far greater things for His children since the beginning of time. The next time you have a prayer or concern, thought or idea, throw them up into God's cloud and watch His will be done!

Power Passage: "Give your burdens to the LORD, and he will take care of you. He will not permit the godly to slip and fall." Psalm 55:22 NLT

Power Point: Allstate, the insurance company, has a slogan. It's "You're in good hands with Allstate." I'm telling you that, "You're in good hands with God." He is perfect in all His ways and loves you more than you know. Whatever concern, worry or issue that you have, give them to Him and trust that He will handle them.

Power Prayer: Dear God, thank You for sending Your son Jesus to die for my sins. Thank You for sitting up high, but listening down low. Thank You for allowing me to have access to You 24/7 through prayer. I'm glad to know that You know what I need before I even ask of it. Help me, God, to spend more time communing with you in prayer. As I grow in You, Lord, help my prayers to be a request for Your will to be done in my life. Give me more of Your Spirit today Father so I can handle the winds of the world. Amen!

DAY 19

GOD CARE

The iCloud isn't the only thing that Apple has created that's impressive. After buying my iPad I noticed that my button at the top was getting stuck from time to time. The button getting stuck really didn't bother me, I never even used it.   Traci suggested that I take it to the Apple store to see if they would fix it, and, if so, how much would it cost. After putting it off for several weeks which is how I normally do things, I decided to go and see what could be done.

Walking into the store, I had a bit of anxiety. I thought that this could end up costing a good bit of money, so I scouted the crowd to find someone who looked extra helpful. Before I could analyze and do my personality profiles on the staff, a store associate asked me how she could help me. I told her what my problem was and she walked me over to the counter to see one of their technicians. At the counter, I informed the technician of the issues and he asked for my name. So, I gave it to him, figuring he was looking me up in the system. He began to play with my device for a bit to assess the problem.

After a few clicks of his computer, he smiled at me and said, "I'll be right back." He took my iPad and went to the back for a few minutes and came back up to the front counter. My first thought was, "Hey dude, where is my iPad?" He opened a white box and pulled out a brand new iPad.

"I'm transferring your information over to this new one," he replied to the question I'd asked in my head.

"What's going on?" I asked him, smiling.

"I'm replacing your iPad," he said. I began to laugh out loud.

"I appreicate that," I laughed, "but why can't you just fix it?"

"You have a service called Apple Care," he said. I gave him a puzzled look and he continued.

"All of our devices have a one-year warranty that covers damages to the device." He reached out to shake my hand and smiled, "Apple takes care of their people."

Wow! For the first time, I really felt proud to be an Apple customer. I'm sure you know where I'm going with this story. How great is our God! Although impressive, neither technology, nor can the man who created it, compare to the power, grace and love of our God above. Just as the Apple company takes care of their customers, how much more does our God take care of His children? There is nothing that we can do, that God can't fix. There is no malfunction or problem within our lives that He can't diagnose and fix. There's no problem too big and grand for Him to handle.

As proud as I felt that day to be an Apple customer, I feel even prouder to be a child of God! He provides for every single one of our needs. And unlike Apple, our warranty with God never runs out! Our protection plan with God is called Grace and Mercy. God gives you Grace every time you wake up in the morning and Mercy every time you sin against him. You can take your broken heart, battered emotions and bruised body to Him, and He will fix you up like new. God cares about the smallest detail of your life! Matthew 6:26 NLT says, "Look at the birds. They don't plant or harvest or store food in barns, for your heavenly Father feeds them. And aren't you far more valuable to him than they are?"

For my iPhone, I have Apple Care, but for my life, I have God Care! We were created in God's image. I can see why a protection plan comes with our life. Today recognize how important you are to God and that He cares for you!

Power Passage: "He heals the brokenhearted and binds up their wounds. He determines the number of the stars and calls them each by name. Great is our Lord and mighty in power; his understanding has no limit." Psalm 147:3-5 NIV

Power Point: There is no problem that God can't fix! He knows us and loves us no matter what has gone wrong in our lives. God's warranty is called Grace and Mercy. He gives us this because He loves and cares for us. You only get one life and body here on Earth, so make sure you take care of it. And don't ever hesitate to take your problems to Him because He can do the impossible in your life.

Power Prayer: Heavenly Father, I just want to say Thank You! You are perfect in all Your ways. Thank You, Lord, for giving me a warranty through Your Son, Christ Jesus. Please make me new today. Thank You for understanding me, and help me to spend more time with You so I can understand You more. Please give me the power of Your Holy Spirit so that I can be used by You today, and give me the boldness, Father, to proclaim Your warranty plan with others. Amen!

DAY 20

CONNECTED TO THE SOURCE

For the past few days, we have been talking about electronic devices and the capacities of them. There is one common thing that must be considered when discussing the convenience and effectiveness of electronics. They all run on power. If I went a whole day without charging my iPad, iPhone and Macbook, they would be powerless. That's right; the power of these devices comes from another source. There is not one electronic device that powers itself. They either need batteries or need to be plugged in to an electrical outlet.

Without power, a device is useless. Once you plug your device into a power outlet, it is able to receive the necessary charge to operate. Your device has storage areas within it that charges and holds temporary power. Without the surge of power from the outlet to replenish the power that has been used, the device is useless.

Have you ever tried to charge your computer by placing it near the outlet? I'm not sure if that will work... What about trying to place your computer near the plug? Will that charge it? I don't think so... Being close just isn't good enough; the device needs to be plugged in to the source of power.

I recently found myself without my cell phone charger and my phone was completely powerless. I was not a happy camper to say the least. I use my phone for so much, personal and work-related, that when the battery dies, I am literally closed for business. My trusty phone that was so helpful at one point, now serves no purpose. No matter how much I want to use it, it's worthless until I can tap into some electrical power.

That's how our lives are. God wants to use us, but if we're not tapped into His holy power, then we are useless. Matthew 19:26 NLT says, "Jesus looked at them and said, 'With man this is impossible, but with God all things are possible.'" I realized this late in my life. I thought I could have true success in life on my own. While outside of God's will, I saw how the worldly success and material things in life went as fast as they came. Believe it or not, you are powerless to your purpose in life if you don't get your daily charge from God's Holy Spirit!

God has a special plan for your life and if you stay connected to Him you will be able to do anything! Philippians 4:13 NIV says, "I can do everything through him who gives me strength." Simple enough right? We start down the wrong path when we try to do things on our own without seeking the power, guidance, and wisdom of God. By not seeking Him, you are saying that you don't need Him. Once He holds back His hand of protection from your life, you will see how imperative it is to stay connected to Him.

You might be wondering, "How can I get my daily charge from the Holy Spirit?" By doing exactly what you're doing now! You get your power by taking time to spend with God in daily prayer and devotion. The more time you spend with Him, the more you become like Him. Once you get your daily charge of His Holy Spirit in the morning, your light will shine bright throughout the day! Get plugged in and let Him use you!

Power Passage: "By his divine power, God has given us everything we need for living a godly life. We have received all of this by coming to know him, the one who called us to himself by means of his marvelous glory and excellence." 2 Peter 1:3 NLT

Power Point: Can you imagine how we, as young people, can be used by God if we allow Him to charge us up with His Power? Get connected to Him throughout the day and keep your battery on full!

Power Prayer: Dear God, thank You for Your availability. Thank You for giving me the means and options to plug into Your power daily. Please give me Your Holy Spirit so that I will want to get my charge from You daily. Once I get my charge, Lord, I give You full permission to use me. Sometimes I might feel like I can't be used, so I'm asking that You will show me how I can be used by You. Jesus, please help me to live everyday with Your power, so I can be a positive influence to others. Amen!

DAY 21

BP OIL SPILL

On April 10, 2010, there was a huge explosion aboard the Deepwater Horizon, a drilling rig in the Gulf of Mexico. The rig was drilling into deep oil reservoirs for BP Oil Company. It was the biggest oil rig explosion in history. It led to the largest accidental oil spill in U.S. history.

The damage from this one explosion was devastating. That day on the Deepwater Horizon, 11 people lost their lives and 17 more were injured. In addition to the humans that lost their lives, thousands of birds, turtles, and mammals also died, while widespread pollution blanketed the gulf coast. Approximately 16,000 miles of coastline in multiple states were affected, including Texas, Louisiana, Mississippi, Alabama and Florida. This has brought long-term damage to our shores and waters and wasted a precious commodity that we depend on in our daily lives.

Oil is one of the most used substances in today's society. From oil, products like Liquefied Petroleum Gas (LPG), gasoline (petrol), diesel fuel, kerosene, jet fuel and fuel oils are made. Most of the substances made from oil are turned into some type of fuel and used to power cars, trucks, or planes. And because we need oil to power our lives, drilling for it, converting it, producing it, and transporting it has created jobs for millions of Americans.

The BP oil spill is a good example of what happens when you have wasted energy and power just floating around. The very thing that had been entrusted to us, to manage and use wisely, brought pain and destruction. What should've brought life to our world, took life from our planet. The power that was used to produce jobs and make dreams come true, now caused vast devastation. Wasted power becomes a hazard!

Look at your life. God has given all of us specific talents and abilities for a reason. The gifts and talents that God has blessed you with will only bring you true success and happiness if you use them for Him. Ephesians 6:10&11NIV says, "Finally, be strong in the Lord and in his mighty power. Put on the full armor of God so that you can take your stand against the devil's schemes." This verse says to be strong in God. Get your strength from Him, and use it for Him.

Take it from me; I spent years of my life using my personality and charm to please myself. I wasted my talents to chase after money, fame, women, success, etc. I hurt and wrongly influenced many people in my younger days. And although I've repented countless times for this, I am still making some past wrongs in my life right…just like BP is still actively cleaning up the gulf.

For years, I was like an oil rig leaking poison to people all around me. I was literally a walking devastation. Now that God has my life under control, He is using me to bring change and hope to others! The great thing is that God wants to do great things in your life, too! There are hundreds of ways to use oil, and there are millions of ways that God wants to use you! All He wants is for us to take the power, talents, personality and gifts that He has given us, and allow Him to shine.

CLICK HERE TO DOWNLOAD

Power Passage: "I pray that from his glorious, unlimited resources he will empower you with inner strength through his Spirit." Ephesians 3:16NLT"

Power Point: How will you be used? Will you allow God to use you to bring encouragement, hope and love to the world? Or will you allow Satan to use you to bring hurt, pain and devastation. You can't serve two masters. Choose today who fuels you!

Power Prayer: Lord, thank You for creating me and for wanting to use me. Help me, Lord, to recognize the power and personality that You have given me. Please, God, show me how to be bold and use it for You, so that I can be an ambassador for You. Please continue to keep me and pour out Your spirit upon me today. I love You, Lord. Amen!

DAY 22

SLAYING YOUR GIANTS

I remember being in the 4th grade at a new school. There were a few bullies in the school that had a way of exerting their powers over me. For whatever reason, they didn't like the attention the new guy was getting. The only thing that kept these big guys off my back was my friend Josh, who was bigger than they were. Everyday Josh would walk me half the way home to make sure I wasn't harmed. It felt good to have someone to watch my back and fight my battles. I can't help but think about how God does this for us, too!

When you think of David and his battle with Goliath, on the surface it seems as if the fight is between a boy and a giant. Look again! It's actually between God and Goliath. Goliath defiled the name of God, so God, through David, had to teach him a lesson. The most impressive thing about this story is David's courage and faith, not in himself, but in God.

1 Samuel 17:40 NLT says, "He picked up five smooth stones from a stream and put them into his shepherd's bag. Then, armed only with his shepherd's staff and sling, he started across the valley to fight the Philistine." The Bible says David chose five smooth stones from a stream of water before going into battle. In the Bible, water represents the Spirit of God, and that tells me that we must have the Spirit of God before we can use the stones God gives us to help us in our daily battles. Let's find out what stones we have to pick up before we go to war!

Stone 1 = God's Holy Word - This is a way of knowing and claiming God's promises.

Stone 2 = Daily Prayer - This gives you direct communion with God.

Stone 3 = Daily Devotion - This allows you to spend time with Him to power up for battle.

Stone 4 = Service - Christ lived a life of service which exemplified humility.

Stone 5 = Praise - God's word says that He inhabits the praise of His people!

As stated in the Bible, David had God's anointing. Sometimes we think that since we are chosen or called by God, life will be easy. This couldn't be farther from the truth. Trials come to all of us, even God's anointed. What's encouraging about this story is that David didn't go from being a shepherd to slaying a giant. David had some pretty impressive victories prior to this ultimate test. 1 Samuel 17:34-36 NIV says, "But David said to Saul, "Your servant has been keeping his father's sheep. When a lion or a bear came and carried off a sheep from the flock, I went after it, struck it and rescued the sheep from its mouth. When it turned on me, I seized it by its hair, struck it and killed it. Your servant has killed both the lion and the bear; this uncircumcised Philistine will be like one of them, because he has defied the armies of the living God." The lion and bear were a test, preparing David for his battle with Goliath. God was building David's faith in Him. This is why trials come. The more we endure and the more God delivers us out of situations, the more faith we have in Him.

I'm sure we're all familiar with the lions and bears of

troubles and trials in our life! They are God's blessings and opportunities in disguise. The thing that often strikes the chords of our deepest fears within us is often the thing that gives us the greatest strength and victory. The lion and the bear that David previously slayed prepared him to slay the giant, Goliath. No lion? No bear? No victory over Goliath! Grab your five stones from the Spirit of God that flows like a river and be prepared for battle!

CLICK HERE TO DOWNLOAD

Power Passage: "And David said, 'The LORD who delivered me from the paw of the lion and from the paw of the bear will deliver me from the hand of this Philistine.' And Saul said to David, 'Go, and the LORD be with you!'" 1 Samuel 17:37 ESV

Power Point: Remember where your strength and power comes from, and then ask yourself, "What is God preparing me to slay?"

Power Prayer: Dear Lord, thank you for another day! Thank you for fighting all of my battles. Help me to learn to lean on You when trying times come. Thank you, Father, for the trying times, for I know that it builds my faith in You. Fill me with Your Spirit today so that I am prepared for the challenges of the day. Amen!

DAY 23

COTTON CANDY

I remember helping a friend at her 5-year-old daughter's birthday party. My assignment was simple—operate the cotton candy machine and keep the kids happy. I thought that this task would be simple. Even though there was a swimming pool, face painting, pizza, and snow cone machine, cotton candy was the most popular. I wonder if I had anything to do with why it was so popular! Probably not; these little kids were going crazy over this sweet treat. I, being a cotton candy specialist, served those little kids with pride. One by one, I dished out sugar on a stick and the kids loved me for it. I remember serving one of my tallest and widest servings of cotton candy to a 4-year-old boy. I sort of felt bad once I gave it to him because it was almost as tall as he was. The little boy ran off excited about the cotton candy experience he was about to have.

The same little boy came back less than five minutes later and asked for more. He also complained that his stomach hurt. This confused me, so I asked him if he was getting the treat for someone else. With his eyes opened wide and pupils dilated he yelled, "No it's for me!" This little guy was demanding more of what was causing him pain. I sat there puzzled, wondering where all of that cotton candy had gone. I would have thought he dropped it or threw it away, if the evidence hadn't been on his face. My young friend ate the cotton candy, and was left with nothing but a tummy ache and a red ring around his mouth.

This reminds me of the enemy, our adversary, Satan. He has a way of making things seems sweet and fun, but those things ultimately cause us pain. His treats turn into tricks and you're left hurting. That little boy had all of that cotton candy and it only lasted him a few moments. When it was gone he had nothing to show for it, but pain and red residue on his face. I've had experiences like that. After nights of drugs, partying, etc., I found myself low and depressed, with nothing to show for the experience but a hangover, empty pockets and low feelings. It's the trick of Satan to give us a temporary fill, and then leave us with nothing but regret to show for the good time we had.

In order for us to live courageous lives for Christ, we must recognize the tricks of the enemy. I found myself for years seeking some fulfillment and trying to quench my internal thirst with things of the world. John 4:14 NIV says, "But whoever drinks the water I give him will never thirst. Indeed, the water I give him will become in him a spring of water welling up to eternal life." God says instead of seeking the world for a quick fix, seek God, for He will fill you up. Not only will He fill you up, but He will also give you everlasting life! Here's a challenge! The next time Satan offers you "cotton candy," no matter how good it may taste, decline it and allow the Lord to bless you and offer you a treat that lasts longer!

CLICK HERE TO DOWNLOAD

Power Passage: "Blessed are those who hunger and thirst for righteousness, for they shall be satisfied." Matthew 5:6 ESV

Power Point: Everything that glitters isn't gold, neither are the things that taste sweet good for you. Stay focused on what really matters in life and pray that God will help you be aware of the tricks of Satan.

Power Prayer: Dear Lord, thank You for another day of life! Please help me not to fall into the devil's traps he has set out for me. There may be things that I am involved in that doesn't please You, if so please take them from me. As I get closer to You, God, help me to have a distaste for sin. Change my mind and heart so that they are in tune with Your will. Amen!

SECTION 4 YOUR GROWTH

DAY 24

HEALTHY SOIL

Have you ever planted a garden before? I'm pretty proud of the experience I've had in a vegetable garden. I'm no expert, but I know that some experience is better than no experience. After building our first home, we had some upgrades and additions added to the house. One of the additions was a brick garden connected to the back of our house I had built for Traci. Traci and I had our first garden, and were so excited about it. We planted tomatoes, peppers, zucchini, squash, and bell peppers. Some came out like the finest grocery store produce, while others needed a little more help. This was an awesome experience, especially since it was our first time in the garden. Okay, I must confess. Traci did most of the gardening, but I was there to assist by pulling up weeds and watering the soil.

We learned early of the importance of healthy soil. We made sure that the area that we used for our garden had healthy soil to assist in the growing of our vegetables. Experts say that the produce that you grow will only be as healthy as your soil, because your fruits and vegetables are pulling its nutrients from the soil.

To have a healthy garden, you must make sure that the soil or dirt is rid of all weeds. You don't want weeds growing in your garden. You also want to make sure that the soil doesn't have too many rocks. Large rocks can get in the way of the roots growing freely. Rotating your crops is another good way to keep a healthy garden and the harvest fresh. Just like people, crops like to eat different things too. Each crop can add something different to the soil it's in. Grow them in different locations and replenish the soil with other crops, and your produce will grow strong and healthy.

Now take a moment and imagine your body and life as a vegetable trying to grow, and your environment and friends as the soil. In order for you to grow in Christ, you have to place yourself in healthy soil. Beware of the large rocks that want to stop you from growing. There may be some friends "weeds" in your life that you need to pull up at the root. If you have people in your life stopping you from growing, then they have no place in your soil. The nutrients in the healthy soil can be viewed as the word of God. If you allow yourself to be in place of weeds and thorns, you will never receive or understand God's word.

Mark 4:7&8 NIV says, "Other seed fell among thorns, which grew up and choked the plants, so that they did not bear grain. Still other seed fell on good soil. It came up, grew and produced a crop, some multiplying thirty, some sixty, some a hundred times." Here, Jesus is talking about the importance of being in good soil. The deeper your soil is, the deeper your roots will grow. The healthier your soil is, the more nutrients your vegetables will get. The more people that you surround yourself with that love Christ, the better you will grow.

Please don't get me wrong; I am not saying to only have super Christian friends. I am suggesting that the people who influence you, while you're growing in this Christian garden, should contribute to your growth. Remember that one of the tips to growing great produce is to switch locations, so don't be afraid to get out of your comfort zone. If you allow Him,

God will come and till your garden. He will keep it fresh and remove the weeds, so that nothing will stop you from growing in Him.

Power Passage: "The seed falling among the thorns refers to someone who hears the word, but the worries of this life and the deceitfulness of wealth choke the word, making it unfruitful. But the seed falling on good soil refers to someone who hears the word and understands it. This is the one who produces a crop, yielding a hundred, sixty or thirty times what was sown." Matthew 13:21-23 NIV

Power Point: Grow your roots deep in the Lord. The deeper you're grounded in Him, the more secure you will be and the taller you will grow.

Power Prayer: Dear Jesus, thank you for allowing me to grow in Your garden of life. Please protect me from the weeds and thorns of life. Please place me in surroundings that will be nutritious to my spiritual growth, and fill me with Your Spirit so that I can grow tall and bear good fruit. Amen!

DAY 25

PLANTED SEEDS

There was once a famous farmer who made a living and became very wealthy owning a successful farm and growing produce. The majority of his harvest throughout his career consisted of vegetables. While in Florida at the National Harvest Federation, he met a young man who specialized in growing oranges. It was the custom at the federation for the farmers to share their crops and harvest with one another; it could lead to the purchase of his seeds or crops. During conversation, the famous farmer tasted one of the young man's oranges and was shocked. He had never tasted an orange so delicious, sweet and fresh. Tasting this sweet orange made him think about his bland cucumbers, squash and other vegetables he was growing back home.

When the famer returned home, he spoke to his wife and all of his workers and informed them that he would stop growing the vegetables that made him rich, and start growing fruit. His wife and staff questioned him about what inspired him to make this drastic change and decision. He said ,"You just need to taste and see the goodness of this fruit! If I'm going to share my crops with the world, I want it to be fruit."

What if I told you that in your own way you're a farmer? That's right, we all sow seeds of some sort with the people we interact with everyday. My only question to you is what type of seeds are you sowing?

Did you know that there is a certain type of fruit that God wants you to plant in His garden called Earth? Galatians

5:22 NKJV says, "But the fruit of the Spirit is love, joy, peace, longsuffering, kindness, goodness, faithfulness, gentleness, self-control. Against such there is no law." The fruits of the Spirit are things that directly reflect the character of Christ. If we all did our jobs, we would have a harvest of love sprouting up all over the earth!

Reflecting Christ's Spirit and character is essential to spiritual growth. It's important that we place ourselves in areas where we can grow ourselves spiritually. And when we do, God can use us to plant seeds of love, joy, peace, longsuffering, kindness, goodness, faithfulness, gentleness, self-control. Psalm 34:8 NLT says, "Taste and see that the LORD is good. Oh, the joys of those who take refuge in him!" Ask yourself if you are producing the type of "fruit" that tastes sweet, or does the fruit you produce leave a bitter taste?

CLICK HERE TO DOWNLOAD

Power Passage: "I am the true vine, and my Father is the gardener. He cuts off every branch in me that bears no fruit, while every branch that does bear fruit he prunes so that it will be even more fruitful. You are already clean because of the word I have spoken to you. Remain in me, as I also remain in you. No branch can bear fruit by itself; it must remain in the vine. Neither can you bear fruit unless you remain in me. I am the vine; you are the branches. If you remain in me and I in you, you will bear much fruit; apart from me you can do nothing." John 15: 1-5 NIV

Power Point: The ONLY way that you can bear the fruits of the Spirit of God is if you're connected to Him! God is the vine from which all of your strength comes from. Stay connected to Him and He will produce sweet fruit through you!

Power Prayer: Heavenly Father, please give me Your power to produce Your fruit! Empower me to sow seeds of love to everyone I come in contact with. Help me bear good fruit so I can reflect Your love and power to Your people. Amen!

DAY 26

POWER OF SUNLIGHT

During the past couple of days we've been talking about spiritual soil, crops and spiritually planting seeds into the world. Let's not forget one of the main components that makes all things grow. Sunlight! Have you ever tried to grow something without light? In an attempt to share with you the importance of the sun and how it affects plants during the growing process, I did a little research.

Plants need the sun because sunlight is made up of electromagnetic radiation, which is given off as energy. The radiation that plants get from the sunlight is the main ingredient in the process called photosynthesis. Photosynthesis is how plants get their energy. Plants convert energy from sunlight into simple carbohydrates. The result of the process? The plant creates food that it can use to grow and stay alive. We would not exist without photosynthesis. Life on planet Earth would not be possible without it. You see, all plants and animals depend on photosynthesis to get their energy. Since animals are dependent on plant life to eat, without photosynthesis, there can be no plant life. And without plant life, there is no animal life. So, not only does our great sun, which is over 90 million miles away and approximately 865,000 miles wide, warm us up and give us light, but it also gives our plant the energy it needs to survive and grow. I guess God knew what He was doing when He said, "Let there be Light!"

My friends, the principle and analogy here is simple. We

cannot and will not grow without the Son, Jesus Christ in our life. He said in John 8:12 NIV "...I am the light of the world. Whoever follows me will never walk in darkness, but will have the light of life." This is the "source of power" we talked about that is needed for getting connected to the source. God has an amazing plan for your life as long as you stay connected to him.

Experts say that plants need a minimum of 6 hours a day of sunlight in order to get the necessary power they need to grow strong. I won't suggest a limit to the time you give Jesus, but I will challenge you to ask yourself whether or not you get enough of His power daily. As bright as the sun shines, Christ wants to shine even brighter in your life so the entire world knows He is abiding in you! The next time you sing. "This little light of mine..." recognize that your light from Christ is bigger than you think!

Power Passage: "Whoever believes in him is not condemned, but whoever does not believe stands condemned already because they have not believed in the name of God's one and only Son. This is the verdict: Light has come into the world, but people loved darkness instead of light because their deeds were evil. Everyone who does evil hates the light, and will not come into the light for fear that their deeds will be exposed. But whoever lives by the truth comes into the light, so that it may be seen plainly that what they have done has been done in the sight of God." John 3:19-21 NIV

Power Point: The Light from Jesus, the Son of God, is all we need to light up the world. While the sun uses photosynthesis to bring power and energy to plants, people should see Christ's "photosynthesis" in our lives as we bring life and light to the world.

Power Prayer: Father in heaven, Thank You so much for giving us Your Son, Jesus Christ, to die for our sins. Help us to show Your character in everything we do. Fill us with Your Holy Spirit so that Your image will bring light to this dark world. Please continue to let Your light shine upon us so that we can grow in You!

DAY 27

RAINY DAYS

On the previous days, we learned that we should place ourselves in positions that will support our spiritual growth. This is what we called healthy soil. We also learned of the importance of planting seeds of love, which are the fruits of the Spirit so that we can bear good fruit for the Lord. Yesterday, we discussed the role of the sun and how it provides power to plants to grow. We compared this concept with the notion that we need to get our power from Jesus, the Son of God, to grow spiritually. The final element I want to discuss in the growth process on Earth, and our spiritual lives is rain.

In 2011, the State of Texas went through one of the worst droughts in U.S. history. With back-to-back days of triple-degree temperatures, residents there were praying for rain. Triple-degree heat and no rain is a deadly combination. Countless vegetation and wild life died due to the lack of rain. Funny how something we complain about can be such a lifesaver at times. What, you never complained on rainy days? I know I have!

The reality about rain is that we can't survive life without it. Rain water helps to replenish our water systems and create healthy soil for growing crops. Rain provides fresh water that allows the rivers to flow, and in return fills lakes and keeps plants alive. Leviticus 26:4 NIV says, "I will send you rain in its season, and the ground will yield its crops and the trees of the field their fruit." We cannot imagine our lives without the rain because it refreshes our land.

What If I told you that the rain and storms within your life were put there for a reason? That's right, just as the trees and plants can't grow without rain, neither can we. We need the Spirit of God to saturate and sustain us. John 7:37-39 NIV says, "On the last and greatest day of the festival, Jesus stood and said in a loud voice, "Let anyone who is thirsty come to me and drink. Whoever believes in me, as Scripture has said, rivers of living water will flow from within them." By this he meant the Spirit, whom those who believed in him were later to receive. Up to that time the Spirit had not been given, since Jesus had not yet been glorified." In this passage, Christ says that He can quench any thirst. Whatever your need is, He will provide.

God loves us so much that He will even allow rain to come in our lives. It is by sending the rain that He perfects our character. Through the power of the Holy Spirit, our test will soon turn unto our testimony! Sometimes, we as Christians, have this preconceived thought that life for us will be perfect, when in reality, it will never be. At least, not on this earth! The next time things get out of hand and it seems like your world is upside down, look up and smile at God. In the words of my grandmother, "God brought you to it, so He can bring you through it."

CLICK HERE TO DOWNLOAD

Power Passage: "For I will pour water on the thirsty land, and streams on the dry ground; I will pour out my Spirit on your offspring, and my blessing on your descendants. They will spring up like grass in a meadow, like poplar trees by flowing streams." Isaiah 44:3&4 NIV

Power Point: The world has a way of drying you out. The dew, the power of the Holy Spirit, is something we must have daily. Just as plants get watered daily, we, too, need the dew of the Holy Spirit daily.

Power Prayer: Our Father and friend, thank You for Your Holy Spirit! Please drench me daily with Your Spirit and saturate my life with Your power. Once I receive Your Spirit, I pray God for the boldness to share You with others I come in contact with. Have Your way within my life, Amen!

DAY 28

THE WORKOUT CALLED LIFE

All this week we have been discussing the power that God has given you, and how to tap into that power. Now that we have a good idea of how to receive the power, you must wonder, "How do I use it?" Practicing the power within you from Christ Jesus is what I call exercising your faith.

I remember working out at the local fitness center in Huntsville, AL. I would see huge body builders in there lifting more iron than I weighed. I always wondered how they progressed to such a high level of fitness. It was comedy as well as motivation for me to see these guys bench pressing and squatting this enormous amount of weight, their veins popping out of their neck. Regardless of how funny they looked, I couldn't deny the fact that they had some of the most sculpted human bodies I had ever seen. For them, going through pain was a part of life. Some of you all didn't catch that. I'll come back to that thought.

The fascinating thing about bodybuilders is that they aren't born that way. I saw a television interview with a guy who had just won a bodybuilding competition. The reporter asked him what motivated him to start lifting weights. The champion bodybuilder then explained to the reporter that being skinny in high school and getting picked on was his motivation. It made me think. Of course, people aren't just born with biceps the size of my waist. Those muscles are

grown and developed through hard work and experience.

The next time I went to the fitness center, instead of wondering how the body builders get to the next level of strength and muscle mass, I decided to ask a guy who was working out near me. This guy reminded me of the actor from the movie, "The Green Mile," Michael Clarke Duncan. He had muscles on top of muscles. I asked this guy how he got so strong and his response was simple, "Pain is weakness leaving the body." He said that from the pain that he experiences today, he would be stronger tomorrow. And that pushed him to work harder, to lift heavier iron, and reach his goals. We talked for a bit more and then I had all the motivation I needed to embark on my journey of fitness.

People ask me all of the time why bad things happen to good people. I believe things happen as a result of the effects of sin; we all have to carry our cross sometimes. Luke 9:23 ESV says, "And he said to all, 'If anyone would come after me, let him deny himself and take up his cross daily and follow me." We will be talked about, cast out and picked on at times just as Jesus Christ was. Think about it. All true Christian are wearing His name so we must expect the persecution. It comes with the title. Paul says this in 2 Timothy 3:10-12 NIV, "You, however, know all about my teaching, my way of life, my purpose, faith, patience, love, endurance, persecutions, sufferings—what kinds of things happened to me in Antioch, Iconium and Lystra, the persecutions I endured. Yet the Lord rescued me from all of them. In fact, everyone who wants to live a godly life in Christ Jesus will be persecuted." In spite of the storms that Paul went through, he continued to preach the gospel of his Friend, Jesus Christ.

Now, to my young friend who might be concerned or afraid, stop those thoughts right now! God promised in

Isaiah 54:17 that no weapon formed against us will prosper! This storm that God has you in right now is for your own good. It says in Romans 8:28 NIV that "All things God works for the good of those who love him, who have been called according to his purpose." Hard times will come, for they are necessary for our growth. Look at the tall trees that have roots just as deep as their height. They wouldn't have gotten to that stature without some rain.

Remember, the bodybuilder I told you about? He also expressed to me the importance of being conditioned for the workout. In order for you to be prepared for the workout that life has in store for you, God has prepared a conditioning plan for your life. Place yourself in surroundings that will be supportive to your growth. Make sure that you plant seeds of love and life into others. Embrace the warmth of our Lord Jesus Christ daily in your life and allow the Him to water you with His Spirit. This is what will prepare you for the workout regiment called life. Be strong!

CLICK HERE TO DOWNLOAD

Power Passage: "But those who hope in the LORD will renew their strength. They will soar on wings like eagles; they will run and not grow weary, they will walk and not be faint." Isaiah 40:31NIV "I can do all things through Christ who strengthens me." Philippians 4:13 KVJ

Power Point: The greater the pain, the greater the gain. God will only give you the test that He trusts that you can pass. When trials come your way, you should feel proud that God trusts you to deal with the circumstances.

Power Prayer: Dear God, thank You for another day. Thank You for the situations in life that make me stronger. Thank You for shielding me from the things, which I cannot handle. Help me to always seek You for my strength and help me to use my power for Your will. Please give me the conditioning to handle whatever comes my way and when I'm victorious I'll give You all of the credit. Amen!

JEREMY J. ANDERSON

DAY 29

DIARY OF A CATERPILLAR

One sunny afternoon, I walked out onto my sunroom and found a caterpillar lying dead, stuck to my tile floor. I instantly had two thoughts. The first was, "Ugh, that's nasty!" The second was, "Man, he didn't even fulfill his purpose in life." You see that caterpillar was born to be a butterfly! I wondered how the caterpillar got in my sunroom in the first place. Wasn't this caterpillar supposed to eventually evolve into a butterfly? The caterpillar, once fully grown secretes a long stream of liquid from its glands called the spinneret. This liquid stiffens forming a silky thread which is used to attach to the end of a twig or leaf. (Once that happens, the caterpillar is stuck to the leaf.) The caterpillar then spins this silky thread around and covers its whole body. The outside layer hardens and forms the cocoon. Inside the cocoon the caterpillar changes into a pupa. In this process, the pupa digests itself from the inside out causing its body to die. The cocoon process can take from 10 days to several months!

During the cocoon process the pupa is getting its strength, and its wings are forming. Once this process is complete, the newly transformed butterfly is ready to emerge from its cocoon. The next phase is my favorite; the butterfly has to push on the walls of the shell until it breaks open! What a fascinating journey. This caterpillar changed from a slow and slimy creature, into a beautiful butterfly!

Look at your life! God didn't create you so you could slowly crawl around hoping not to get stepped on. He created you to soar! You just have to go through your transformation before you can get your wings.

Caterpillars and butterflies are so different, but the transformation they go through is so beautiful. We're going to take a look at how we can apply their metamorphosis to our transformation through Jesus Christ.

We can learn a lot from this process.

1. Just as the caterpillar gets stuck to the twig or leaf to start its process, we, too, must get stuck to the Lord!

2. Just as the caterpillar spins its silky thread covering its body, we, too, must be filled and covered with the Spirit of God!

3. Just as the pupa causes its own body to die, we, too, must die daily of self, from the inside out!

4. If you're in your own cocoon, embrace the struggle. For like the pupa, this is where you will get your strength and the power to flap your wings! Isaiah 40:31ESV says, "But they who wait for the LORD shall renew their strength; they shall mount up with wings like eagles; they shall run and not be weary; they shall walk and not faint."

5. Just like the caterpillar, we all have different time frames of transformation. For some the process is quick, for others it may take some time, so don't get discouraged.

6. Do you want to be made new and free from your cocoon? Do you want to spread your wings and fly? Then you must "PUSH" your way out! "Pray Until Something Happens."

Keep on "pushing" and soon you will spread you wings

and fly! Let us fly high above the ground where we once crawled! Let us soar through the air giving praises to God! As the sun shines through our new wings, let there be a rainbow of color and hope on the ground for other caterpillars to see! Though created to be, not all caterpillars make it to become butterflies. The one lying dead in my home didn't...will you?

Power Passage: "Therefore if any man be in Christ, he is a new creature: old things are passed away; behold, all things are become new." 2 Corinthians 5:17 KJV

Power Point: If you change your thinking, you will change your mind, and once you change your mind, you will change your life.

Power Prayer: Father in Heaven, Thank You for life! Thank You for not giving up on me. Please, Lord, make me new every day so that I can get closer and closer to You! Give me wings so that I can soar to new heights. Help me to evolve from the sinful life that I have so that I can embrace righteousness through You! Amen!

DAY 30

STARVE THE FLESH & FEED THE SPIRIT

One of my favorite sports is boxing. My favorite part of a boxing match, second to the fight itself, is when the two contestants stand toe to toe and their height, weight, arm length, and their winning and losing percentages are displayed for an in-depth comparison. From this point, I can gauge who might be favored to win the match. Although in boxing, size doesn't always matter, it's a fact that the closer the contestants are in height and weight, the better the fight will be.

Could you imagine having two boxers almost identical in their size, height and arm lengths, but starving one for two weeks prior to the fight? It's pretty obvious that the starved boxer would be too weak to even stand a chance against the boxer who was fed continuously. That's because nutrition is fundamental to the growth of us all. If you put good in, you'll get good out.

Look at your spiritual life. No matter where you are in your journey, you can get better. That right, regardless of your addictions, sins, or your struggles you can be successful in this fight for your salvation! When it comes to Christianity, I have lived the roller coaster lifestyle for most of my life. One day I'm up, and the next day I'm down. One day I'm standing for Christ, the next day, I'm looking for an excuse to trip and fall. I got to the point when I was just plain tired—

tired of falling for the enemies tricks, tired of the devil picking on me and tired of letting God down. A friend of mine once told me that when you really want change, you will change.

I know that at times it seems hard to change, but in order for you to be successful and implement real change, you have to know where this battle is taking place. The boxing match for your soul salvation takes place in the mind. That's right, your brain is Madison Square Garden and the two contestants battling for the title of your life are your flesh and your spirit. These are two natures that battle daily within your mind and put up a constant struggle. Romans 7:22-24 NLT Paul says, "I love God's law with all my heart. But there is another power within me that is at war with my mind. This power makes me a slave to the sin that is still within me. Oh, what a miserable person I am! Who will free me from this life that is dominated by sin and death?"

Paul states here in Romans that there is even a battle within his own mind competing for domination. Then he asks, "Who will free me from this life that is dominated by sin and death?" This flesh and spiritual side that Romans talks about is real. We were naturally born with the nature of sin. Psalm 51:5 NLT says, "For I was born a sinner yes, from the moment my mother conceived me." I praise God for the promise in 2 Corinthians 5:15. "This means that anyone who belongs to Christ has become a new person. The old life is gone; a new life has begun!" That's right; you can be born again! Just because you are baptized and you join the church doesn't mean you are completely free from sin. Satan will work even harder in your life to make you fall to his tricks of sin. Don't give him the upper hand.

You might ask how we give him the upper hand. Let's take a look at the boxers again. Remember we discussed that a fed boxer would definitely be victorious against a starved one? In order for you to win in this fight for your life, you must starve your flesh, feed your spirit. This might be how your mind works if you feed your spirit and your flesh:

- Half of you wants to go to church, the other half wants to sleep in.
- Half of you wants to give, the other half wants to keep.
- Half of you wants to read the Bible, the other half says it's boring.
- Half of you wants to be patient, the other half is in a hurry.
- Half of you wants to forgive, the other half wants vengeance.
- Half of you wants to witness, the other half wants to keep silent.
- Half of you wants to love, the other wants to hate.

You might be wondering how to starve the flesh side. For starters, you have to watch what you put into your mind. Really analyze the type of TV shows you watch. Are these shows that are supportive and reflective to the type of Christian lifestyle you wish to live? What about the music you listen to? Music is one of Satan's oldest tricks. He had amazing musical abilities in heaven! Look at the type of music that you listen to and the message behind it. If it doesn't reflect Christ's character, then it's pulling you from Him. Only after I cut the secular music from my playlist was I able to hear God clearly. Another way to starve the flesh is by keeping your temple holy. God wants to dwell within your body. Physical pollutants like drugs, nicotine, alcohol, etc. block your spiritual receptors, which also draws you away from connecting with God.

Feeding the Spirit is actually quite simple. Let's start with daily prayer in the mornings, evenings, and even throughout the day. You can even whisper a prayer while you're in school or at work. You don't always have to be so formal with God. Just make sure that when you pray, you are honest with God (since He knows the truth anyway) and make sure it comes from your heart. I once heard a preacher say, "Prayer is the lifeline to the throne room of grace."

Daily devotion and Bible study are also critical ways to feed your spiritual side. Spend as much time with Jesus as possible. By spending time with Him, we take on His true character. Service is another great way to feed the spiritual side within you. The Bible says, "faith without works is dead." Christ lived a life of service. Find ways that you can serve in your church or community. By following this simple action plan of starving the flesh and feeding the spirit, you will find yourself growing strong in Christ. If God be for you, who can be against you? When the announcer says, "Let's get ready to ruuuumble," who will win the boxing match of your salvation?

Power Passage: "So I say, let the Holy Spirit guide your lives. Then you won't be doing what your sinful nature craves. The sinful nature wants to do evil, which is just the opposite of what the Spirit wants. And the Spirit gives us desires that are the opposite of what the sinful nature desires. These two forces are constantly fighting each other, so you are not free to carry out your good intentions." Galatians 5:16-17 NLT

Power Point: The point here is simple; if you want to have a real, long lasting and fruitful relationship with Christ then you have to starve the flesh and feed the Spirit within you! God is not going to force Himself upon you. He wants you to give yourself to Him. In the words of Forever Jones, "He wants it All!"

Power Prayer: Father, I need You! There is no way that I can fight this battle without You! You have already made a way of escape from the penalties on my sins. Help me to follow that path. There is a war going on for my salvation. Help me to have the courage and strength to starve the flesh and feed the Spirit. Thank You for making Your Holy Spirit available for me and fill me up every day so that I can unlock the power that You have placed within me. Amen!

JEREMY J. ANDERSON

Author, Public Speaker, Mentor, Youth Counselor

Book Jeremy Anderson for your next event!
Need a speaker who will Educate, Enlighten & Encourage your Church, Organization, Youth, or Group?
Jeremy's has made ministry his life by traveling and speaking. His passion is reaching out to others from all walks of life to help them find their inner Prodigy.

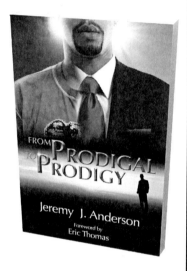

For booking or more information, contact: 256-759-7492
Prodigal2Prodigy@gmail.com
29806 Park Hill Dr. Madison, AL

You can also order Jeremy's book, "From Prodigal To Prodigy." Purchase online @ www.jeremyandersonm.org or www.spiritreign.org

SPIRIT REIGN
COMMUNICATIONS & PUBLISHING

Thanks to all of you who have been so supportive of our company. As we grow in grace, we hope and pray that you will continue this journey with us. We have many plans on the table for where we would like to see Spirit Reign in the future. Without the support of clients and customers such as you, that will never happen. We want you to continue to enjoy our products and publications. Feel free to shoot us an e-mail at spiritereign@ mindspring.com with suggestions on how we can make our company the best ministerial resource development company possible. May God continue to richly bless you.

Sincerely,

Daryl S. Anderson Sr.
Founder / CEO
Spirit Reign
Communications & Publishing

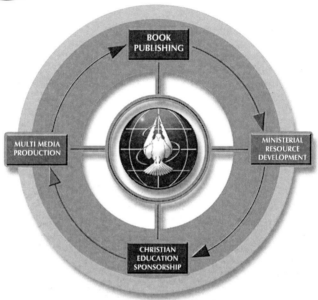

Spirit Reign Communications and Publishing was established to produce quality Christ-centered presentations in a variety of mediums. Our commitment to excellence is manifested in the published works, ministerial resource materials, products and services we provide for our clients and customers. We have been blessed with an innovative team of visionary thinkers whose business and creative prowess distinguish our company in a unique and positive way. Whether in traditional print, electronic books, or audio and visual recording, we effectively communicate the word of God in the 21st century with contemporary slants on the age-old gospel. Among the ministries we are associated with, we are proud sponsors of "Families At The Alter Ministries," and "The Prodigy Plan" founded by Daryl S. Anderson Sr., and P2P 'Prodigal 2 Prodigy," founded by Jeremy J. Anderson. We offer professional art and design services for promoting or creating individual corporate identity of Christ-centered institutions.

SPIRIT REIGN

COMMUNICATIONS & PUBLISHING

Here are some of our top titles:

The Secret To Success: by Eric Thomas
From Prodigal To Prodigy: by Jeremy J. Anderson
7 Principles of Atonement: by Daryl S. Anderson Sr.
Ever Rising and Total Trust During Trying Times: by Katie
A. Arnette

For information on publishing opportunities for authors visit
us online @ www.spiritreign.org